Celebrating Friendship

Celebrating Friendship

An anthology compiled by
Brian Frost and Pauline Webb

EPWORTH PRESS

Selection and arrangement
© Brian Frost and Pauline Webb 1986.

See also the *Sources and Acknowledgements*
section, which forms an extention
of this copyright notice.

British Library Cataloguing in Publication Data

Celebrating friendship: an anthology.
1. Friendship—Literary collections
I. Frost, Brian   II. Webb, Pauline
808.8'0353   PN6071.F7

ISBN 0-7162-0426-6

First published 1986 by
Epworth Press
Room 195 1 Central Buildings
Westminster London SW1H 9NR

Typeset at The Spartan Press Ltd,
Lymington, Hants
and printed in Great Britain by
Richard Clay
Bungay, Suffolk

Contents

Preface

Celebrating Friendship is an anthology in praise of a widespread but little-sung human experience.

There have been many to praise erotic love; patriotic devotion gets a good press; but few have celebrated the joys of friendship determined neither by sex nor by devotion to a common cause, but simply arising from mutual affinities and shared delights.

Friendship is difficult to define, but we have found echoes of it in aphorisms drawn from many different cultures. It is a gift to be celebrated in song and story and enjoyed in shared hospitality. It has its demanding side too, as the sections on the candour and conflict possible in friendship illustrate. It is personified in people from many different walks of life, portrayed in cameos depicted by their friends. Above all, friendship has the divine imprint upon it, and in shared faith develops a profound and everlasting quality.

We hope this anthology evokes the comfort friends bring, reinvigorates our friendships and anticipates a time when the whole community will seek to become a 'society of friends'.

Personally we offer this collection to the many people who have enriched our lives, especially to David Killick, a lifelong friend of Brian's, and as a tribute to the memory of Margaret Shaw, who for Pauline epitomizes all that friendship means. We offer it, too, to Theo and Helen Kotze, friends we both share, who give so many people encouragement and support through their gift for making friends.

BRIAN FROST   PAULINE WEBB

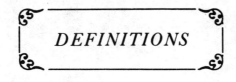

DEFINITIONS

1   A friend is one to whom one may pour all the contents of one's heart, chaff and grain together, knowing that the gentlest of hands will take and sift it, keep what is worth keeping and with the breath of kindness blow the rest away.

    Arabian proverb

2   Friends are an aid – to the young, in keeping them from making mistakes; to the old in supplying their wants and doing for them what in the failure of their physical powers they cannot do for themselves; to those in the prime of life by making it possible to get fine achievements brought to accomplishment.

    Aristotle

3   A friend is, as it were, a second self.

    Cicero

4   Friendship adds a brighter radiance to prosperity and lightens the burden of adversity by dividing and sharing it.

    Cicero

5   Friendship – one heart in two bodies.

    Joseph Zabara

6   True friends are those seeking solitude together.

    Abel Bonnard

7   Friendship is the inexpressible comfort of feeling safe with a person, having neither to weigh thoughts nor measure words.

    Jeremy Taylor

8   By friendship you mean the greatest love, the greatest usefulness, the most open communication, the noblest sufferings, the severest truth, the heartiest counsel, and the greatest union of minds of which men and women are capable.

Jeremy Taylor

9   True friendship will disdain no office as too mean, decline none as too difficult. It will not only take, but seek all opportunities of doing good and reward itself with the delight and pleasure of such kind employment.

Feast Day Sermon at St Mary-le Bow 1684

10 A true friend inbosoms freely, advises justly, assists readily, adventures boldly, takes all patiently, defends courageously, and continues a friend unchangeably.

William Penn

11 Friendship is a disinterested commerce between equals; love an abject intercourse between tyrants and slaves.

Oliver Goldsmith

12 The feeling of friendship is like that of being comfortably filled with roast beef; love like being enlivened with champagne.

Samuel Johnson

13 Friendship is a sheltering tree.

Samuel Taylor Coleridge

14 A friend is a poem.

Persian proverb

15 I find friendship to be like wine, raw when new, ripened with age, the true old man's milk and restorative cordial.

Thomas Jefferson

16 Friendships begin with liking or gratitude – roots that can be pulled up.

George Eliot

17 A friend may well be reckoned the masterpiece of nature.

Ralph Waldo Emerson

18 Friendship needs no words – it is solitude delivered from the anguish of loneliness.

Dag Hammarskjold

19 In Gujarati, which is my mother tongue, we have a word 'Lehnoo' which it is almost impossible to translate into English. The nearest equivalent would be a combination of attraction and affinity of spirit, and that does seem to me to be a wonderful description of an essential part of the meaning of friendship.

Nadir Dinshaw

20 Friends are in a sense a mirror, a repository of your own past actions and qualities.

John Kasmin

21 A best friend is someone you don't feel guilty about not phoning.

John Kasmin

22 It's the friends you can call up at 4 a.m. that matter.

Marlene Dietrich

23 You have a lot of friends who love you dearly and you don't know who they are.

Shelley Winters

24 They are not quite my friends, but I know them better than many who are; they aren't related to me, but they might as well be. They are the close friends of my close friends – my friends-in-law.

Katharine Whitehorn

25 A friend is one who knows all about you and loves you just the same.
A friend is one who steps in when all the world has gone out.

Entries in an autograph album

26 Friends are, above all, the family we choose for ourselves.

Jill Tweedie

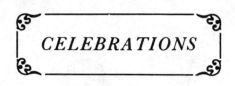

CELEBRATIONS

1

Here's to you old friends
May you live a thousand years
Just to keep things happy
In this vale of tears
And may I live a thousand years
Just short one day
'Cos I wouldn't care to stay on earth
When you had gone away.

Found on a calendar

2

My lovely friends
How could I change
towards you who
are so beautiful.

I ask you, Sir, to
stand face to face
with me as a friend
would; show me the
favour of your eyes.

Sappho

3

'Tis hard to find in life
A friend, a bow, a wife,
Strong, supple to endure,
In stock and sinew pure,
In time of danger sure.

False friends are common. Yes, but where
True nature links a friendly pair
The blessing is as rich as rare.
To bitter ends

9

You trust true friends,
Not wife nor mother
Not son nor brother
No long experience alloys
True friendship's sweet and supple joys;
No evil men can steal the treasure;
'Tis death, death only, sets a measure.

From the Panchatantra

4   To love one's friends is to love one's own good.

Aristotle

5   They seem to take the sun from the heavens who take friendship from life, for we receive from the immortal gods no better or more delightful boon.

Cicero

6   All kinds of things rejoiced my soul in their company – to talk and laugh, and to do each other kindnesses; to read pleasant books together; to pass from lightest jesting to talk of deepest things and back again; to differ without rancour as a man might differ with himself; and when, most rarely, dissension arose, to find our normal agreement all the sweeter for it; to teach each other and to learn from each other; to be impatient for the return of the absent and to welcome them with joy on their homecoming; these and suchlike things, proceeding from our hearts as we gave affection and received it back, and shown by face, by voice, by the eyes, and by a thousand and other pleasing ways kindled a flame which fused our very souls together, and, of many, made us one.

Augustine of Hippo

7   At night I dreamt I was back in Ch'ang-an;
         I saw again the face of old friends,

And in my dreams, under an April sky,
They led me by the hand to wander in the Spring winds.
Together we came to the ward of Peace and Quiet;
We stopped our horses at the gate of Yüan Chên.
Yüan Chên was sitting all alone;
When he saw me coming, a smile came to his face.
He pointed back at the flowers in the western court;
Then opened wine in the northern summer-house.
He seemed to be regretting that joy will not stay;
That our souls had met only for a little while,
To part again with hardly time for greeting.
I woke up and thought him still at my side;
I put out my hand; there was nothing there at all.

Po Chü-i

8   Let not a thousand friends seem too many in your eyes.

Solomon Ibn Gabirol

9   No recipe openeth the heart but a true friend, to whom you may
impart griefs, joys, fears, hopes, suspicions, counsels, and
whatsoever lieth upon the heart to oppress it . . . This com-
municating of a man's self to his friend works two contrary
effects, for it redoubleth joys and cutteth grief in halves . . . For
there is no man that imparteth his joys to his friends but he
joyeth the more, and no man that imparteth his griefs to his
friend but he grieveth the less . . . For friendship maketh indeed
a fair day in the affections from storm and tempests, but it
maketh daylight in the understanding out of darkness and
confusion of thoughts.

Francis Bacon

10   These are my friends in whom I more rejoice
Than doth the King of Persia in his crown.

Christopher Marlowe

11 There can be no friendship where there is no freedom. Friendship loves a free air, and will not be fenced up in straight and narrow enclosures.

William Penn

12 When a friend asks there is no tomorrow.

George Herbert

13

      Should auld acquaintance be forgot,
      And never brought to min'?
      Should auld acquaintance be forgot,
      And auld lang syne?

      For auld lang syne, my dear,
      For auld lang syne;
      We'll tak a cup o' kindness yet,
      For auld lang syne.

      And here's a hand, my trusty fiere,
      And gie's a hand o' thine!
      And we'll tak a right guide-willie waught
      For auld lang syne.

Robert Burns

14

      I have known sorrow, therefore I
      May laugh with you O friend
      more merrily
      Than those who never sorrowed
      upon earth,
      And knew what laughter's worth.
      I have known laughter, therefore I
      May sorrow with you far more
      tenderly
      Than those who never knew how sad a thing

Seems merriment to one's
heart-suffering.

Source unknown

15   Is it so small a thing
To have enjoyed the sun,
To have lived light in the spring,
To have loved, to have thought, to have done;
To have advanced true friends, and beat down baffling
foes?

Matthew Arnold

16   Two sturdy oaks I mean which side by side
Withstand the winter's storm,
And spite of wind and tide
Grow up the meadow's pride
For both are strong.

Above they barely touch, but undermined
Down to their deepest source,
Admiring you shall find
Their roots are intertwined
Insep'rably.

Henry Thoreau

17   I awoke this morning with devout thanksgiving for my friends,
the old and the new. Shall I not call God the Beautiful who daily
showeth himself to me so in his gifts? I chide society, I embrace
solitude, and yet I am not so ungrateful as not to see the wise,
the lovely and the noble-minded as from time to time they pass
my gate. Who hears me, who understands me, becomes mine, a
possession for all time. Nor is nature so poor but she gives me
this joy several times and thus we weave social threads of our
own, a new web of relations; and, as many thoughts in
succession substantiate themselves, we shall by and by stand in
a new world of our creation, and no longer strangers and

pilgrims in a traditionary globe. My friends have come to me unsought. The great God gave them to me.

Ralph Waldo Emerson

18 We two boys together clinging,
    One to the other never leaving,
    Up and down the roads going, North and South excursion making;
    Power enjoying, elbows stretching, fingers clutching,
    Arm'd and fearless, eating, drinking, sleeping, loving,
    No law less than ourselves owning, sailing, soldiering, thieving, threatening,
    Misers, menials, priests alarming, air breathing, water drinking, on the turf or sea-beach dancing,
    Cities wrenching, ease scorning, statues mocking, feebleness chasing,
    Fulfilling our foray.

    Walt Whitman

19 And a youth said, Speak to us of friendship
    And he answered, saying
    Your friend is your needs answered.
    He is your field which you sow with love and reap with thanksgiving
    And he is your board and your fireside.
    For you come to him with your hunger and you seek him for peace.

    When your friend speaks his mind you fear not the 'nay' in your own mind.
    Nor do you withhold the 'aye',
    And when he is silent your heart ceases not to listen to his heart;
    For without words, in friendship, all thoughts, all desires, all expectations are born and shared, with joy that is unacclaimed.

    When you part from your friend, you grieve not;

For that which you love most in him may be clearer in his absence, as the mountain to the climber is clearer from the plain.

And let there be no purpose in friendship save the deepening of the spirit.

For love that seeks aught but the disclosure of its own mystery is not love but a net cast forth; and only the unprofitable is caught.

And let your best be for your friend.
If he must know the ebb of your tide, let him know its flood also.
For what is your friend that you should seek him with hours to kill?
Seek him always with hours to live.
For it is his to fill your need, not your emptiness.
And in the sweetness of friendship let there be laughter and sharing of pleasures.
For in the dew of little things the heart finds its morning and is refreshed.

Kahlil Gibran

20
Everything that God does
Has its portion of sun;
Every thorn has its rose,
Every sad night its dawn.

For the meadow there's hay,
For the field the harvest;
For the air th' eagle gay;
Gives the bush for the nest.

The tree has its verdure,
Every bee its honey,
Rolling waves, its murmur,
Every low tomb, a sky.

In this world, where all lower

To some higher point tend,
For the branch there's the flower,
And for the heart, the friend.

J. K. Aggrey

21   Friend, whatever hardships threaten
If thou call me,
I'll befriend thee,
All-enduring, fearlessly,
I'll befriend thee.

The Oglala Sioux Indians

22   I owe so large a debt to life,
I think if I should die today
My death would never quite repay
For music, friends and careless laughter,
The swift, light-hearted interplay
Of wit on ready wit, and after,
The silence that most blessed falls
Across the room and firelit walls
And quells our flame of jesting strife.
I owe so large a debt to life
No gift can wipe it quite away,
Nor any tears that I can borrow
From watching all the world's wide sorrow,
As Autumn never can allay
The promise of a sunlit morrow
We had as legacy from May.

Winifred Holtby

23   From quiet homes and first beginning
Out to the undiscovered ends,
There's nothing worth the wear of winning
But laughter and the love of friends.

Hilaire Belloc

24   Today has it all, sunshine
      snow to the north, the lake
      frozen over, the Sunday leisure
      of friends, a silence like

      a seizing up of the megamachine,
      a forgetting of towns,
      Broken pieces of ice skipped
      over ice sing no tunes

      but hit one high sweet note
      each time they touch the ice,
      hold the note to its twittering death
      halfway over the lake. Wild geese

      are frozen in attitudes, improbably
      secure from the fowler. Nothing forages.
      Five of us and a happy dog
      alone now on the crisp ridges.

      The barrowed dead live for us,
      we banish fear of raucous change
      to this moorland, this
      Wales, dismiss the sly danger

      with laughter, love, attention
      to now, as given us by all
      our senses, the sight, the sound,
      the feel, the taste, the ice-sweet smell

      of a cerulean winter's day
      on water, skin and grass
      now we are together and absolute
      in this moment of grace.

Gwyn Williams

25   friend –
          it was great meeting you again
          after 30 incredible years

we last met when you were 15

but you don't seem 45

you are 15
made up to look 45

Michael Macnamara

26   Like the shade of a great tree in the noonday heat is a friend.
Like the home port with your country's flag flying after a long
journey is a friend. A friend is an impregnable citadel of refuge
in the strife of existence. It is he that keeps alive your faith in
human nature, that makes you believe that it is a good universe.
He is the antidote to despair, the elixir of hope, the tonic for
depression . . . Give to him without reluctance.

Anonymous

27   Hold a true friend in both hands.

Nigerian proverb

28   And blessed be friends and comrades:
Blessed be Rolfe in his dark house and the hearts of friends,
Blessed by the loud continuous sea: Naomi.
Blessed on their mountains under the enshrouding shine of the
    spent starlight: Don and Charlie:
With their wives, children, heirs and assigns.
Blessed, blessed
In the waste lots and the burning cities of man's estate,
Fishers by still streams, hunters on the hard hills, singers,
    dreamers and makers:
Blessed be all friends
With their wives, husbands, lovers, sons, daughters, heirs and
    assigns
Forever.

Thomas McGrath

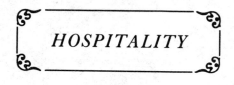

HOSPITALITY

1   The ornament of a house is the friends who frequent it.
    Ralph Waldo Emerson

2   We never know a friend until we have stayed in his house.
    German Proverb

3   My old friend prepared a chicken with millet,
        Inviting me to visit his country home,
        Where the green of the trees
        Girdles the village
        And beyond the walls the blue hills begin.

        We opened your windows to inspect the kitchen-garden,
        Took some wine, and spoke of mulberries and flax.
        Wait until the Autumn Festival:
        I shall come again,
        to enjoy your chrysanthemums.

    Meng Hao-jan

4   In human life, friends so rarely meet –
        Their motion like the morning and evening stars.
        This night – how wonderful a night,
        When we share the same candle-light!
        How long can youth and strength remain?
        We are turning grey already at the temples
        We discover half our friends have died –
        The shock sickens us inwardly.

        We little guessed it would be twenty years
        Before I came again into your hall.
        When last we parted

21

You were still unmarried.
Look at you now with this row of boys and girls
Who merrily pay me respect –
Their father's friend,
And ask me where I come from.

Long before the questioning has ended
The children spread a feast for me, with wine:
Spring leeks gathered in the night rain,
Freshly steamed rice sprinkled with millet.
You plead – 'Another meeting may be hard:
Down with ten cupfuls in a single bumper!'
Ten cups even cannot make me drunk:
I glow with the sense of our old affection.

Tomorrow a mountain will divide us,
Our separate futures
Engulfed by the world's affairs.

Tu Fu

5   Old friends, but parted by river and sea,
       Divided many a time by stream and hill,
       We suddenly meet, amazed, suspect we are dreaming,
       Lament with each other, ask how the years have passed.
       Cold shines the rain in the beam of our single lamp;
       Drifting mists muffle the dense bamboos.
       Feeling tomorrow's grief again before us,
       We pass from hand to hand the 'parting cup'.

Ssu-k'ung Shu

6   Tonight, grave sir, both my poor house and I
       Do equally desire your company;
       Not that we think us worthy such a guest,
       But that your worth will dignify our feast
       With those that come; whose grace make that seem
       Something, which else could hope for no esteem.

It is the fair acceptance, sir, creates
The entertainment perfect, not the cates.
Yet shall you have, to rectify your palate,
An olive, capers, or some better salad
Ushering the mutton; with a short-legged hen,
If we can get her, full of eggs, and then
Lemons, and wine for sauce; to these a coney
Is not to be despaired of, for our money;
And though fowl be scarce, yet there are clerks,
The sky not falling, think we may have larks,
I'll tell you of more, and lie, so you will come! . . .

Ben Jonson

7
I saw a stranger yestreen
I put food in the eating place,
drink in the drinking place,
music in the listening place,
and in the sacred name of the Triune
He blessed myself and my house,
my cattle and my dear ones,
and the lark said in her song
often, often, often,
goes the Christ in the stranger's guise.

Kenneth Macleod

8
We shook hands,
    but between us
Stood race and history
    and a jealous present

Even in that brief grasp
I felt our two negatives recoil
    from meeting;
each sensing the discomfort
of the unyielding silence

23

which was the mark
   only
of our defeat.

We shook hands and lingered there
with that firm clasp
of happy meeting,
cqual joy to the visitor as to the visited
and sitting leisurely down
we smiled and sighed our greetings
dipping our fingers
   into the groundnuts
we shared.

David Williams

9   To the degree to which our loneliness is converted into solitude,
we can move from hostility to hospitality.
   . . . The real host is the one who offers that space where we do
not have to be afraid and where we can listen to our own inner
voices and find our own personal way of being human.

Henri Nouwen

10   Ours yet not ours, being set apart
        As a shrine to friendship,
        Empty and silent for most of the year,
        This year awaits from you
        What you alone, as visitor, can bring,
        A weekend of personal life.

        In the house backed by orderly woods,
        Facing a tractored, sugar-beet country,
        Your working hosts engaged to their stint,
        You are unlike to encounter
        Dragons or romance; were drama a craving
        You would not have come.

Books we do have for almost any
Literate mood, and notepaper, envelopes,
For a writing one (to 'borrow' stamps
Is a mark of ill-breeding):
Between lunch and tea, perhaps a drive;
After dinner, music or gossip.

Should you have troubles (pets will die,
Lovers are always behaving badly)
And confession helps, we will hear it,
Examine and give good counsel:
If to mention them hurts too much,
We shall not be nosey.

Easy at first, the language of friendship
Is, as we soon discover,
Very difficult to speak well, a tongue
With no cognates, no resemblance
To the galamatias of nursery and bedroom,
Court rhyme or shepherd's prose,

And, unless spoken, soon goes rusty,
Distance and duties will divide us,
But absence will not seem an evil
If it makes our re-meeting
A real occasion. Come when you can:
Your room will be ready.

In Tum-Tum's reign a tin of biscuits
On the bedside table provided
For nocturnal munching. Now weapons have changed,
And the fashion in appetites:
There, for sunbathers who count their calories,
A bottle of mineral water.

Felicissima notte! May you fall at once
Into a cordial dream, assured
That whoever slept in this bed before

Was also someone we like,
That within the circle of our affection
Also you have no double.

W. H. Auden

11 What splendid children's parties we had! All the Kremlin
children would be asked, twenty or thirty of them. There were a
lot of people living in the Kremlin and all of them were on easy,
straightforward terms . . .

I remember my last birthday party while my mother was still
alive. It was February 1932, and I was six years old. The
Kremlin apartment was filled with children. We recited verses
in Russian and German and satirical couplets about stock-
workers and political double-dealers. We danced the Ukrainian
gopak in folk costumes we'd made ourselves out of coloured
paper and stiff cotton netting. Artyom Sergeyev, a friend of my
brother Vasily and now a much decorated general, crouched on
all fours in a bearskin and growled while somebody read a fable
by Krylov. The audience screamed with delight. The walls were
festooned with the drawings and wall newspapers we had made.
Later the whole crowd, parents and children alike, went to the
dining room for tea and cake and candles. My father was there
too. He was only watching, of course, but it amused him. Once
in a while he enjoyed the sounds of children playing.

Svetlana Alliluyeva

12 Above my table three magnolia flowers
Utter their silent requiems.
Through the window I see your elms
In labour with the racking storm.
Giving it shape in April's shifty airs.

Up there sky birds from a brew of cloud
To blue gleam, sunblest, then darkens again,
No respite is allowed
The watching eye, the natural agony.

Below is the calm a loved house breeds
Where four have come together to dwell
– Two write, one paints, the fourth invents –
Each pursuing a natural bent
But lose through nature's formative travail
Then each in his own humour finding the self he needs.

Round me is all amenity, a bloom of
Magnolia uttering its requiems,
A climate of acceptance. Very well
I accept my weakness, with my friends'
Good natures sweetening every day my sick room.

C. Day-Lewis

13   . . . The holidays arrived. I knew that, like most of the other
students, my young rescuer, Mohamed Fauzy, wanted to learn
to speak English perfectly. So I went to his house to suggest that
he used his holidays to take lessons in town.
'Have you eaten?' asked his mother.
'Oh, I've already had a bean sandwich.'
'You must have something to eat with my husband.'
On a small round table she set out a simple meal: aubergines
with tomatoes, raw onions, lettuce leaves. It was three o'clock.
She wouldn't be eating anything, she explained, because she
had already had her meal, but she brought in some salt. She
took a piece of bread, dipped it in the salt and put it in her
mouth.
'Now we are friends for ever,' she said with a smile. 'We have
shared bread and salt.'

Sister Emmanuelle

14   We put on our annual pantomime last week to puzzle the
natives: candles burning all over the garden, a modest show of
fireworks, some assorted concoctions of the grape and the grain,
and I told my only funny story . . .

You may well ask why a long-lasting humanist like myself gets steamed up about a pagan festival which can hardly have much metaphysical importance for me. The answer is simple: my wife would, I think, claim to be a fair-to-middling believer in the serious aesthetics of her ancestral faith, and is even fonder of giving parties. Most thoughtful Indians firmly believe that if the goddess Lakshmi existed for anything at all it was for the giving of parties.

. . . Our small party had been chosen at random from our locals, our neighbours, our personal mates of long-standing; we had not, any more than we ever have, the remotest idea of choosing an ethnic or social mix. It was well towards the end of supper that someone did a swift ethnic analysis of the chums around the table.

We were: English, Scottish, Irish, Jewish, Muslim, Zoroastrian, Hindu, Catholic, Protestant. And I suppose me.

I must insist that all this came about by the merest chance. If it had been fixed as some sort of social experiment, it would have been unforgiveable. It was an unexpected fluke, and had it not been for the odd guesswork of one of the friends, would never have even been noticed.

So one up for Lakshmi, goddess of fortune.

James Cameron

15   Then I saw the earth blazing with sunlight:
I saw children laughing as they learned the secrets of the earth
    From people who smiled who shared their knowledge:
I saw the world celebrating carnival – black and white,
    Protestant and Catholic, Christian and Jew,
    All joining hands and dancing through the countryside
    And the city streets.
I saw the streets a mass of colour
    Where people left their jobs and houses to join the fun:
And then I saw people returning to jobs
    Where they felt the fulfilment of creation.

I saw faces full of peace and joy,
I saw children full of food and excitement;
I saw prisons with open doors for people to come out,
And I saw homes with open doors for people to enter in.
I saw beauty at every street corner
And heard music in every home.
I saw people discussing religion in bus queues,
And politics in the tube.
I saw babies on the knees of old men,
While their parents danced.
I saw green grass, free from litter,
And trees full of birds.
I heard people singing as they cleaned the pavements:
I saw houses, strong and shining with new paint.
I saw each family with a home of their own
And friends to share it.
I saw people free: to love and be loved, to give and to receive.
I saw peace in people's hearts, joy in people's eyes
And a song on everyone's lips.
I saw dreams being dreamt
    And lights shining in the darkness:
I saw water in the desert
    And fire in the mountains:
I felt warmth in the winter-time
    And heard laughter in the rain:
And I saw a pound note in the gutter
    That nobody had bothered to pick up.

Alison Head

CANDOUR

1   Just as yellow gold is tested in the fire, so is friendship to be tested by adversity.

Ovid

2   It is only the friendship of the good that is proof against evil tongues; hardly will a man be brought to believe anything discreditable about the friend whose loyalty has been proved by himself through many a year and never been found wanting. Such friends have perfect trust in one another and are incapable of doing each other wrong, and have all the qualities that are confidently expected in true friendship. But in the less genuine kind the caluminous whisper may easily prove fatal.

Aristotle

3   Between friends there is no need of justice.

Aristotle

4   Thou hast describ'd
        A hot friend cooling. Ever note, Lucilius,
        When love begins to sicken and decay,
        It useth an enforced ceremony.
        There are no tricks in plain and simple faith . . .

William Shakespeare

5   The friends thou hast, and their adoption tried,
        Grapple them to thy soul with hoops of steel;
        But do not dull thy palm with entertainment
        Of each new hatch'd, unfledg'd comrade. Beware
        Of entrance to a quarrel; but, being in,
        Bear't that th' opposed may beware of thee.

Give every man thine ear, but few thy voice;
Take each man's censure, but reserve thy judgment.

William Shakespeare

6　I can defend myself from my enemies, but not from my friends.

Honein Ben Isaak

7　Opposition is true Friendship.

William Blake

8　Friendship cannot exist without Forgiveness of Sins continually.

It is easier to forgive an enemy than forgive a Friend.

William Blake

9　I have tried to make friends by corporeal gifts, but have only
Made enemies. I never made friends but by spiritual gifts,
By severe contention of friends and the burning fire of thought.

William Blake

10　Do be my Enemy – for Friendship's sake.

William Blake

11　There is something frightening about the sight of a friend: no
enemy can be so terrifying as he.

Girodano Bruno

12　He makes no friend who never made a foe.

Alfred, Lord Tennyson

13　If we would build on a sure foundation in friendship we must
love our friends for their sakes rather than for our own; we must
look at their truth to themselves, full as much as their own truth

to us. In the latter case, every wound to self-love would be a cause of coldness; in the former, only some painful change in the friend's character and disposition – some fearful breach in his allegiance to his better self – could alienate the heart.

Charlotte Brontë

14 In the matter of friendship, I have observed that disappointment here arises chiefly, not from liking our friends too well, or thinking of them too lightly, but rather from an over-estimate of *their* liking for us and opinion of *us*.

Charlotte Brontë

15 Friends are as dangerous as enemies.

Thomas De Quincey

16 Better be a nettle in the side of your friend than his echo.

Ralph Waldo Emerson

17 I wish that friendship should have feet, as well as eyes and eloquence. It must plant itself on the ground, before it vaults over the moon.

Ralph Waldo Emerson

18 Every man should have a fair-sized cemetery in which to bury the faults of his friends.

Mark Twain

19 Enemies publish themselves. They declare war. The friend never declares his love.

Churton Collins

20 If I had to choose between betraying my country and betraying my friends I hope I should have the guts to betray my country.

E. M. Forster

21   A man's friend likes him but leaves him as he is; his wife loves him and is always trying to turn him into somebody else.

    G. K. Chesterton

22   If you want a friend you must be willing also to wage war for him; and to wage war, you must be capable of being an enemy.

  You should honour even the enemy in your friend. Can you go near to your friend without going over to him?

  In your friend you possess your best enemy. Your heart should feel closest to him when you oppose him.

    Friedrich Nietzsche

23   Friends are God's apology for relations.

    Hugh Kingsmill

24   God gave us our relatives: thank God we can choose our friends.

    Ethel Watts Mumford

25   I thank Thee for my friends, so sweet and kind, so much wiser and stronger than I. I don't deserve a single one of them. Make me a doormat for their feet, a willing target for their wit, a sponge for their good advice, a trumpet for their interesting deeds. They must think a great deal of me, or they would not be so determined to rule my life for me. Make me humble and grateful.

    David Head

26   One of the principal functions of a friend is to suffer (in a milder and symbolic form) the punishments that we should like, but are unable to inflict, upon our enemies.

    Aldous Huxley

27   Go to hell.
       When you go
       I shall bolt the door behind you.
       Seven bolts, without a safety-catch, as in the rifle
       You carried on your shoulder,
       Will bristle from the door, torture-nails in your eyes.

       You will go down
       Crooked stairs, leading to a long-forgotten tower
       And wonder how far you are gone
       And remember you have already known
       This very day, long ago.

       Go to blazes.
       My spirits are low like yours.
       But your world is better off in its grey shroud
       While I am cowed,
       Tearing the cover of my world into ragged bands
       With my bare hands.

       I don't want you in my guts any more.
       You are too much my own sore.
       Too bloody earnest,
       Far too close
       You can take it from me:
       Go to hell. Leave me be.

       Maxim Ghilan

28   Friend and your flatterer I cannot be.

       Seventeenth-century English proverb

29   We must never allow the joy of friendship to become self-
       regarding, at any rate for long. The true joy lies in the mutual
       quest, not in the momentary pleasure which the mirror offers.

       Max Plowman

30 Friendship with oneself is all important because without it one cannot be friends with anyone else in the world.

Eleanor Roosevelt

31 I wonder sometimes if I have been unfaithful in my friendships; so many have come and gone, not through any active breach or loss of kind feeling, but from the fact that we have each become different people: and as we became different our points of intimate contact have diminished ... The real test of the genuineness of a friendship, when circumstances have brought about separation, is whether one does or does not regret that the friendship was ever formed. In very few of my friendships has that sense of regret followed; over all the rest, when the period of intimacy has ended, I have retained a lively feeling of gratitude for benefits received, and to some whom I never now meet or even hear from, my thoughts go constantly, still registering the old affection of the days when meeting was an exciting pleasure and parting always a regret.

Laurence Housman

32 The more we come to realize the extent of the penetrating influence which our own hidden life and the hidden life of our friend exert upon each other, the more acutely do we come to appreciate how inadequately prepared we are to listen, no matter how mature we may be ... all the deepest friendships ultimately bear within themselves the seeds of tragedy unless both persons have their lives open to a power that is infinitely greater and purer than themselves.

Douglas Steere

33 There comes a moment, at least in my experience of friendship, when a barrier has been broken through. What do I mean by this? I mean there comes the moment when we have put ourselves so deeply into the recesses of the other person's personality that we are vulnerable, we are within their grip, as it

were, but we do not seem to mind it at all. We have trusted the other person with ourselves and they have trusted us with themselves. There are now no areas in their lives or ours where the sign 'Keep off' can now be placed. A true and trusty friend very rarely tramples over the personality of the other. He treads very gently and keeps clear because he does not have to know everything about the other person. Such trust results in warmth and love and mutual happiness and mutual joy.

Ivor Smith-Cameron

34 The motivating cause in all true friendship can surely never be anything but the joy and the pleasure which the friendship engenders, and the desire for the other person's good. Yet here we enter what appears to be a paradox – for surely one of the most obvious products of a friendship must be that there is no one from whom we can ask more than from our closest friends. Yet the paradox is only a seeming one, for whilst it is perfectly true that we can and indeed should ask anything from our friends, it is just as true that this, though a very important characteristic of friendship, is nevertheless a by-product of it – it is not and must never become its chief end.

Nadir Dinshaw

35 Though one can have many friends, only a few can be close . . . When it comes to friendship we can spread ourselves too thin. An intimate friendship implies a sharing, not only of interests, but of values and the baring of one's inner self which is always a risk.

Mary O'Hara

36 I could take the distance
When miles between us lay.
I felt that we were still good friends
Five hundred miles away.
But I can't take the distance

I see in your eyes today.
Oh, please, Jackie,
Please don't go away.

The miles that lay between us
Were something I could bear
But there's a different kind of distance
In the look that you now wear.
And I feel that we are far apart,
Though you're standing now right there.
Oh, please, Jackie,
Tell me you still care.

Carole Etzler

37

I loved my friend
He went away from me.
There's nothing more to say.
The poem ends,
Soft as it began –
I loved my friend.

Langston Hughes

38 They say a clean cut heals soonest. There's nothing sadder to
me than association held together by nothing but the glue of
postage stamps. If you can't see or touch or hear a man, it's best
to let him go.

John Steinbeck

39

Don't walk before me,
I may not follow;
Don't walk behind me,
I may not lead;
Just walk beside me
and be my friend.

Albert Camus

LOVE

1 Friendship is love without his wings.

French proverb

2   Love is like the wild rose-briar,
      Friendship like the holly tree –
      The holly is dark when the rose-briar blooms
      But which will bloom most constantly?

      The wild rose-briar is sweet in spring,
      Its summer blossoms scent the air;
      Yet wait till winter comes again
      And who will call the wild-briar fair?

      Then scorn the silly rose-wreath now
      And deck thee with the holly's sheen,
      That when December blights thy brow
      He still may leave thy garland green.

Emily Brontë

3   Being her friend, I do not care, not I,
      How gods or men may wrong me, beat me down;
      Her word's sufficient star to travel by,
      I count her quiet praise sufficient crown.

      Being her friend, I do not covet gold,
      Save for a royal gift to give her pleasure;
      To sit with her and have her hand to hold
      Is wealth, I think, surpassing minted measure.

      Being her friend, I only covet art,
      A white pure flame to search me as I trace
      In crooked letters from a throbbing heart,
      The hymn to beauty written on her face.

John Masefield

4   My friend, my bonny friend, when we are old,
            And hand in hand go tottering down the hill,
        May we be rich in love's refined gold,
            May love's gold coin be current with us still.

        May love be sweeter for the vanished days,
            And your most perfect beauty still as dear
        As when your troubled singer stood at gaze
            In the dear March of a most sacred year.

        May what we are be all we might have been,
            And that potential, perfect, O my friend,
        And may there still be many sheafs to glean
            In our love's acre, comrade, till the end.

        And may we find when ended is the page
        Death but a tavern on our pilgrimage.

John Masefield

5   Such love I cannot analyse;
                It does not rest in lips or eyes,
                Neither in kisses nor caress,
                Partly, I know, it's gentleness.

                An understanding in one word
                Or in brief letters it's preserved
                By trust and by respect and awe
                These are the words I'm feeling for.

                Two people, yes, two lasting friends,
                The giving comes, the taking ends.
                There is no measure for such things,
                For this all Nature slows and sings.

Elizabeth Jennings

6 What wind brings to the lagging sail
Rain to the drooping flower,
Sweet fire
And the broken bread
And song's peace
To the lonely hour,
You bring
And blithely, to your kind
You come, and lo!
The sail is spread,
The flower dances in the sun,
The heart leaps heavenward
Like flame –
And God is in the broken bread.

Harry Lee

7 The road by the shore garden looms dark.
The lamps are yellow and fresh.
I am very calm. Only do not
talk to me about him.
You are sweet and true – we will be friends . . .
Walk around, kiss, grow old . . .
And light months will fly past
like the snowy stars above us.

Everything promised him to me:
the sky's faded, scarlet rim,
sweet dream on Christmas Eve,
the many-sounding wind at Easter,
the red vine shoots,
waterfalls in the park,
two large dragon flies
on the rusty iron fence.

I could not but believe
that he would be friends with me,

as I walked the hill slopes
on the hot stone path.

Anna Akhmatova

8   When snow lies covering the roads,
And makes the roof its floor,
I'll start out for a walk – and see
You standing at the door;

Alone, in your autumnal coat,
Bare-haired, bootless, you stand:
You struggle with your thoughts, and chew
The damp snow in your hand.

Far out into the distant dark
Trees, fences fade away:
Alone amid the falling snow
Disconsolate you stay.

The water from your scarf rolls down
Your sleeves and lingers there:
Like morning dew the little drops
Now sparkle in your hair.

And suddenly a shining wisp
Of hair lights up your face:
It tints your scarf, your shabby coat,
Your finger's fragile grace.

The snow is wet upon your lashes,
There's anguish in your eyes,
But every feature of your face
Is a unique surprise.

As with an iron chisel
Dipped in antimony,
So clearly on my heart are you
Engraved undyingly.

And in it will for ever live
Your eyes' humility;
Be then the hard world merciless –
It has no claims on me.

And therefore this wide night of snow
Resolves itself in two;
I cannot draw the frontiers
Dividing me from you.

But who we are, and whence are we,
When of those long years' space,
Only the idle words are left,
And of us not a trace?

Boris Pasternak

9

I suddenly have come to love
You who have been no more than friend
So long and constantly . . .
                              I am
A traveller startled that the end
Of stormy questing in a ship
for lands of mystery should be
to sight the blue smoke of his home
and anchor at his native quay.

George Buchanan

10

Do not forget old friends
you knew long before I met you
the times I know nothing about
being someone
who lives by himself
and only visits you on a raid

Leonard Cohen

47

11

You were my friend
before you married me
But now I am too close
for you to see.
Together, we're alone.
From far away
you write in letters what
you never say.
By separation
you are blind no more.
From Manchester you love me
as before.

Sydney Carter

12 Maybe we have to learn a new language, or several of them, like
the ones which Sister Lea learned. She helped found our Girls'
School in Thessaloniki and later went to India to work with
leprosy patients there as a Greek Orthodox nun. When
questioned by a visiting Bishop if she had learned the 'language
of the natives' she hesitated for a moment and then replied, 'Oh
yes, Your Grace, I learned five of them –
The language of smiling,
The language of weeping,
The language of touching,
The language of listening
And the language of loving.'

Bruce Lansdale

13

Our friendship has its seasons
and it crests and troughs like summer in Karachi.
At first there is the gentle light
prolonged sungaze over the soft earth:
the blue sky seen so clear so long
time extends as the days lengthen
there's more to do each day than ever could
Our friendship opens season in this way.

Suddenly the heat becomes unbearable
and one rages with one's skin
at the flimsiest of clothes:
the artificial coolnesses multiply;
each below-zero cold drink
shrivels up the throat leaving
it as unquenched as ever.
You emerge often as a nymph –
it seems the summer has a
skin shedding effect leaving
you barely beautiful – and then
in one day of intense dust
the clouds gathering roll over
and rain unprecedented
freshens the twilight and the air smells earthy.
Our friendship has its seasons, as I said.

Summer cools its heated fury
and as parched lips reach for
a kiss of water and love
there's space created in us
in between us and as the
morning recedes no more and
daylight fills the soft eyes without hurting
our friendship changes season as I learn.

Abbas Husain

14 Friendship is a serious affection; the most sublime of all affections. In a great degree, love and friendship cannot subsist in the same bosom; even when inspired by different objects they weaken or destroy each other, and for the same object can only be felt in succession. The vain fears and fond jealousies, the winds which fan the flame of love, when judicially or artfully tempered, are both incompatible with the tender confidence and sincere respect of friendship.

Mary Woolstonecraft

15 Once when modern literature was the subject of conversation, my brother (who it must be remembered had very little use for erotic feelings) said to one of his pupils: 'Why is the tiresome theme of love between the sexes always taken as the motive of all novels?' 'But what other feeling could cause the same conflicts?' asked the student thoughtfully. 'Why, friendship, for example!' answered my brother vivaciously. 'Friendship has quite similar conflicts but upon a much higher plane. First, there is the mutual attraction caused by sharing the same views of life, and then the happiness of belonging to one another and forming mutual plans for the future. Furthermore, there is the mutual admiration and glorification. A sudden distrust is awakened on one side, doubts arise as to the excellence of the friend and his viewpoints on the other side, and finally the consciousness is borne in upon both that the parting of the ways has been reached, although neither one feels himself ready for this renunciation. Does all this not represent unceasing conflicts, carrying with them suffering of the most intense character?'

The student looked dubious and it was evident that he had never dreamed that friendship could be so passionate.

Friedrich Neitszche

16 Nothing so enriches erotic love as the discovery that the Beloved can deeply, truly and spontaneously enter into friendship with the friends you already had: to feel that not only are we two united by erotic love, but we three or four or five are all travellers on the same quest, have all a common vision.

C. S. Lewis

17 All of life is a putting together of fragments of love to try to re-create the wholeness of our earliest experience of love. A search for something lost − something lost when we left the fluid warmth of the womb, for the very price of our birth is loss of security, and in leaving the closeness of our mother's arms we are learning that all growth must be loss before it is gain . . .

And for you as a child – do you remember? When you left the safety of mother was your first love for a doll, or an animal, or the companionship of someone imaginary perhaps but perfectly fitted to your own needs? . . . Believing someone loves you is the root of self-confidence, the beginning of being able to love others. And when you meet a real child, trust is already established. As one little girl said, 'My friend is black and I am pinkish, but we both have the same voice.'

Elizabeth Hannon

18 Friendship, however begun, is a voyage of discovery, full of perils and surprises. As the friends have intercourse, which deepens into that fullness of mutual trust, which is implied in their union, they learn more of one another, are startled, perhaps by finding unexpected defects, and cheered by unveiling unrealized powers, but as the cementing force of community in hopes and interests tells on them increasingly, their original venture of faith finds consecration in experience.

Herbert Hensley Henson

19 Friendship has something universal about it. It consists in loving a human being as we should be able to love each soul in particular of all those who go to make up the human race.

Friendship which is pure, like the love of our neighbour, has in it something of a sacrament.

Simone Weil

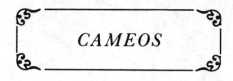

CAMEOS

1   No man set a higher value on friendship than Johnson. 'A man,' he said to Reynolds, 'ought to keep his friendships in constant repair' or he would himself be left alone as he grew older. 'I look upon a day as lost,' he said later in life, 'in which I do not make a new acquaintance.' Making new acquaintances did not involve dropping the old. The list of his friends is a long one, and includes, as it were, successive layers, superimposed upon each other, from the earliest period of his life . . .

The record of his contests in this kind fill a large space in Boswell's pages. That they did not lead to worse consequences show his absence of rancour. He was always ready and anxious for a reconciliation, though he would not press for one if his first overture was rejected. There was no venom in the wounds he inflicted, for there was no ill-nature; he was rough in the heart of the struggle, and in such cases careless in distributing blows; but he never enjoyed giving pain. None of his tiffs ripened into permanent quarrels and he seems scarcely to have lost a friend.

Leslie Stephen on Samuel Johnson

2   There was never any question at any time of Jane Austen teaching many things solemnly. Children enjoyed her company and she enjoyed theirs largely because they amused each other. She was equally at home with adolescents and as ready to enter their thoughts and feelings. Edward's daughter Fanny was fifteen years old, pretty, dark-eyed, animated and enthusiastic. She and her Aunt Jane immediately took to each other. Fanny poured out her aspirations and hopes, Jane listened with amusement and growing affection. It was the start of a relationship that was later to mean a great deal to her. 'Almost another sister!' she exclaimed to Cassandra. 'I would not have supposed a niece would ever have been so much to me, she is

quite after one's heart.' It was the first time Jane had tasted the pleasures of friendship with someone of a younger generation.

Lord David Cecil on Jane Austen

3   But, of all the intimacies formed at this time by Mr Pitt, there was none that ripened into more cordial friendship than that with Mr Wilberforce. The son of a banker at Hull, the owner of a good estate in Yorkshire, William Wilberforce, though born in the same year as Pitt, was sent three years later to Cambridge. There the two young men were but slightly acquainted, but, at the General Election of 1780, Wilberforce was, after a sharp contest, returned for the town of Hull, and meeting Pitt in the House of Commons and in social circles, they rapidly grew friends.

Earl Stanhope on William Pitt

4   Sometimes I fancy an immense separation, and sometimes, as at present, a direct communication of Spirits with you. That will be one of the grandeurs of immortality – There will be no space and consequently the only commerce between spirits will be by their intelligence of each other – when they will completely understand each other – while we in the world merely comprehend each other in different degrees – the higher the degree of good, so higher is our Love and friendship . . . The reason why I do not feel at the present moment so far from you is that I remember your ways and manners and actions; I know your manner of thinking, your manner of feeling; I know what shape your joy or your sorrow would take; I know the manner of your walking, standing, sauntering, sitting down, laughing, punning and every action so truly that you seem near to me. You will remember me in the same manner – and the more when I tell you that I shall read a passage of Shakespeare every Sunday at ten o'clock – you read one at the same time and we shall be as near each other as blind bodies can be in the same room.

John Keats to his brother

5 His acute sense of enjoyment gave such relish to his social qualities that probably no man, not a great wit or a professional talker, ever left, in leaving any social gathering, a blank so impossible to fill up. In quick and varied sympathy with, in real adaption to every whim or humour, to help in any mirth or game, he stood for a dozen men. His versatility made him unique. What he said once of his own love of acting applied to him equally when at his happiest among friends he loved, sketching a character, telling a story, acting a charade, taking part in a game; turning into comedy an incident of the day, describing the last good or bad thing he had seen, re-producing in quaint, tragical or humorous form and figure some part of the passionate life with which all his being over-flowed.

John Forster on Dickens

6 I have lost in her the warmest and dearest friend surely a man ever had. Why this noble and tender spirit should have had such bounty for me and should have so freshened my advancing years, my absorbed and divided mind, I cannot tell. But I feel, strange as it may sound, ten years older for her death . . . None will fill her place for me.

William Gladstone on the Dowager Duchess of Sutherland

7 I knew him well and am proud to have been his friend. He has become the symbolic figure of his age, which he summed up completely. He made dying Victorianism laugh at itself and what serious reformers had laboured for years to accomplish he did in a moment with a flash of an epigram; gaily, with humour and wit for his weapons.

Richard Le Gallienne on Oscar Wilde

8   We were friends and have become as strangers. But it is best so and we will neither conceal nor draw a veil over it as if we had any cause to be ashamed. We are like two ships, each of which has its own course and its own goal; it may be that our paths may cross again and that we shall celebrate a feast-day together as we did in the past when the gallant ships lay in one harbour and under one sun, as if their common goal had already been reached. But then came a time when we were driven far apart by the inexorable power of one another, so great will be the change that the various suns and seas have wrought in us! The law governing our lives has decreed that we should live henceforth as strangers; but just by reason of this, we shall become more sacred to one another. The stars, apparently, follow some immense, invisible curve and orbit, in which our so widely varying courses and goals may be comprehended as so many little stages along the way. Let us elevate ourselves to this thought. Our lives are too short and our powers of vision too limited to permit us to be friends other than in our stellar friendship; even though doomed to be enemies here on earth.

   Frederich Nietzsche on himself and Wagner

9   I cannot attempt to describe my uncle. Many can do that so much better than I. I am dominated and absorbed by his greatness. He seems to me as rich and large as the world. I am lost in his depth, silenced by his nobility. I remember his words to me about great things: 'Be silent about great things; let them grow inside you. Never discuss them: discussion is so limiting and distracting. It makes things grow smaller. You think you swallow things when they ought to swallow you. Before all greatness, be silent – in art, in music, in religion: silence.' And so before him I must be silent and let him speak for himself:

   'I want to make the most of whatever light people have got, however slight it may be, to strengthen and deepen whatever they already possess, if I can . . . Christianity taught us to care.

Caring is the greatest thing, caring matters most.' These seem to me his last most final words, uttered in a voice so small and still and far away, it seemed hardly his own.

Gwendolene Greene on Friedrich von Hügel

10   Like all passions, Freud's friendship was both generous and unjust, violent and extravagant, fertile and pregnant with misunderstandings, even conflicts for the two parties concerned. In addition, it was interested, in the higher as well as in the common meaning of the word. Freud, it seems, needed to be indebted to his friends in some way; and his debt was not only intellectual, for his material circumstance, always precarious and sometimes desperate, often obliged him to accept, if not ask for financial help. He has explained that, at first, he found the idea of borrowing from his friends extremely painful; but Hammerschlag, who was very poor himself, managed to persuade him that there was nothing humiliating about it, that material help from his closest friends was simply a mark of confidence in his future success . . .

Marthe Robert on Sigmund Freud

11   What Toni Woolf meant to Jung on that perilous journey (coming to terms with his feminine -anima) can perhaps best be summed up by something he told me towards the end of his life. He was carving in stone, which had become his favourite visual medium, some sort of memorial of what Emma Jung and Toni Woolf had brought to his life. On the stone for his wife he was cutting a Chinese symbol meaning 'She was the foundation of my house.' On the stone intended for Toni Woolf, who had died first, he wanted to inscribe another Chinese character to the effect that she was 'the fragrance of the house'. The imagery of meaning of this ancient Chinese ideogram is a direct visual expression and part of the symbolism of an element in the human spirit which informs it of what,

59

though still far off and invisible, is inevitable and leads him towards it.

Laurens van der Post on Carl Jung

12 Bloomsbury was an almost unique phenomenon in our cultural history and has been greatly misunderstood. Efforts will no doubt continue to be made to force it into one or other familiar category – as a movement or a salon or a school. It is none of those things. It was simply a group of lifelong, like-minded friends who happened to differ in outlook from their contemporaries. The very word Bloomsbury in this sense conceals as much as it reveals. The essential characteristic of the group of people to whom the name was applied was mutual sympathy and understanding: it was almost – but not quite – the only shared characteristic. The other quality they had in common was applying reason to all aspects of life, including those in which emotion or sensibility are dominant, and the intellectual insight which enabled them to do so. They did not accept, because they did not find it reasonable to do so, that there were large areas of life in which convention had the force of law. They broke the rules when they thought them stupid.

A. L. Gadd on The Bloomsbury Group

13 Since Winifred died, many people have wondered where exactly her genius for friendship lay. It came, I think, from an instinctive skill in the art of human relationship which most of us acquire only after years of blunder and quarrelsome pain. St John Irvine has said that he saw her radiance in other people, and this is undoubtedly true. But it is also true that few individuals are jet black or even neutral grey; most of them possess their own radiance, their peculiar glamour, if the beholder's eye is benevolent enough to discern it. Winifred realized that the desire to be good is a fundamental part of each normal person's make-up. It may be overlaid by pessimism, camouflaged by cynicism, transformed by bitterness, but the

observer who perceives it beneath the trappings can usually count on a gracious response.

Vera Brittain on Winifred Holtby

14 One of the most amusing events of my life occurred when I took the chair for a private celebration of Belloc's sixtieth birthday. There were about forty people assembled, nearly all of them what is called important in the public sense, and the rest were even more important in the private sense, being his nearest intimates and connections. To me it was that curious experience, something between the Day of Judgment and a dream, in which men of many groups known to me at many times all appeared together as a sort of resurrection . . . It was to be, and was, a very jolly evening; there were to be no speeches. Only I, as presiding, was to be permitted to say a few words in presenting Belloc with a golden goblet modelled on certain phrases in his heroic poem in praise of wine, which ends by asking that such a golden cup should be the stirrup-cup of his farewell to friends:

> And sacramental raise me the divine
> Strong brother in God's last companion, wine . . .

. . . Certain fragmentary words, a memory of a late Victorian poet, Sir William Watson, floated on the surface of my mind; and it was those words that I should have said if I had said anything. For what the poet said to his friends is all that I could have added, in a merely personal spirit to the many things that were said that night about Hilaire Belloc; and I should not have been ashamed if the words had sounded like a vaunt:

> Nor without honour my days ran,
> Nor yet without a boast shall end;
> For I was Shakespeare's country man,
> And were not you my friend?

G. K. Chesterton on Hilaire Belloc

15 When you found her you discovered something very rare – a heart at leisure from itself, which is the rarest of all virtues, that of

humility, not thinking badly about yourself, but not thinking about yourself at all. Everything was immediately referred to God. 'Anything you found in my letters was probably put there by yourself and by God. I don't feel I had anything to do with it, just passing on things I had been taught.' She seemed to be immediately ready to become en rapport with you, and without explanations to see your point of view and be completely at your service. This characteristic is what all her friends emphasize. Like Christina Rossetti, of whom this remark was made, 'she was replete with the spirit of self-postponement', and she might truly have made her own the words of Sir Thomas Browne, 'There is no man that apprehends his own miseries less than myself, and no man that so nearly apprehends another's.'

Lumsden Barkway on Lucy Menzies

16 Kingsmill is the only human being I have ever known in whose company I never suffered one moment of boredom; whose solid figure I never saw looming up, and whose voice I never once heard, except with unalloyed happiness. I first met him in Manchester in 1929, when I was working there on *The Guardian* . . . Intimacies cast their shadows before them; they begin in advance of acquaintanceship. This is why the first sight of someone who will be dear to one is never as a stranger. Love originates in a past too remote to be measured and is projected into a future likewise immeasurable. You take someone's hand, look into their eyes, even in certain cases enfold them in an embrace before you know, or even think to ask, their name.

Thus, when I saw Kingsmill coming to the barrier at Manchester Central Station I at once knew him, and began talking to him as an intimate. Thenceforth we went on so talking, on and off, until he died twenty years later, almost to the day.

Malcolm Muggeridge on Hugh Kingsmill

17 Charlie Andrews remained the unique individual who had stepped out of his position as a foreigner, a stranger to India, into

the lives and hearts of Indians in order to show that nationality and race were infinitely less important than brotherhood and love. Many other Englishmen gave their lives to India. Some lived as Indians. None quite acquired his gift of being an interpreter, more trusted by 'the others' than by his own people. He gave all he had to give; and as he gratefully acknowledged, he received richly, in return.

Hugh Tinker on C. F. Andrews

18 The central preoccupation of his life, it was plain to see, was friendship and he had a rather special attitude towards friendship. He never casually dropped friends, as most people do, out of forgetfulness, or through change of circumstances – though he might drop one with perfect deliberateness if the friend had offended him in some vital way: and when this happened, he was unforgiving. Otherwise, if someone became a friend, he might expect to remain so for life, though gravitating over the years from one grade of his friendships to another. He believed literally, as more than a sentimental cliché, that the true history of the human race was the history of human affection. And for this reason it was a principle with him to keep his friendships in mind and to be continually reflecting on them. Also to the end of his life, he was on the lookout for new friends and showed great enterprise in finding them.

P. N. Furbank on E. M. Forster

19 As a companion Studdert Kennedy was a sheer delight, for he was a wholly loveable person. His laugh was a thing of joy, and his smile had a never-to-be-forgotten radiance. He would sit in an armchair smoking endless cigarettes and drinking countless cups of tea, while he thrilled us with his wisdom and magnetic humour. His was the humour of one who laughs and makes jokes for the fun of it, and not merely for the purpose of evangelization, though he could use it in every direction with equal irresistibility. To go to the theatre with him was to have

your attention removed from the stage to the companion at your side who was laughing and chortling with enjoyment. Then suddenly, at a touch of pathos in the play, those wonderful eyes would grow large and sad, and he was not ashamed of letting tears fall down his cheeks.

H. R. L. Sheppard on Studdert Kennedy

20   Tillich's genius for presence was especially present in his personal relationships. Once during my second year at the seminary, when I did not yet know him except as my professor, I happened to be coming down the Broadway hill beside the Columbia campus and saw him walking up the west side of the street. It was autumn. He was without the beret he generally wore in lieu of a hat, coatless, his grey jacket blowing in the wind. He gestured to me, so I crossed the street. As we met he immediately began – 'What you said at the student meeting yesterday was very important. You were rightly cautious. Now tell me what you *really* think.' He took my arm and turned me round so that I would accompany him a little way toward the subway station. And for the next five minutes we were deep into an interesting conversation.

Rollo May on Paul Tillich

21   Bonhoeffer spent in all five months in Munich and Ettal. It was his first separation from Bethge since their friendship had ripened, and the extent to which he had come to depend upon it appears vividly from the letters to Bethge which have been preserved; one gains the impression from the extant half of the correspondence that Bethge was less dependent upon close contact than was Bonhoeffer. Bonhoeffer's power in human relationships was such as to render him almost invariably dominant, but in this exceptional friendship he both was, and was not the stronger. Bethge combined an outstanding depth and range of response with a quiet integrity which would never

be taken by storm. That Bonhoeffer valued this, a passage from one of the letters shows:

'You have endured the weight of this friendship, especially heavy because of my demanding nature (which I myself detest and of which, happily, you have again and again reminded me,) with great patience and without becoming embittered. . . '

Mary Bosanquet on Dietrich Bonhoeffer and Eberhard Bethge

22 Courtesy is a weak word with which to try to convey that outgoing friendliness of his, that made those with him feel that they were the people he most, at that moment, wanted to see, and their concerns the things he most wanted to hear of. It was, I suppose, that quality more than any other that drew people to him. His understanding and interest were so real that he in some measure and quite genuinely took the colour, chameleon-like, of those he was with . . . This comprehension joined with his tact and humour to make him the perfect peace maker among discordant elements; he could always throw a bridge when gulfs yawned. He had every gift for running a mixed team, and a very mixed team his Peace Pledge Union members were; he was probably himself the only person who understood all their various points of view and angles of approach . . . His sanity and undogmatic humour salted all gatherings where he was; he was an idealist with his feet firmly planted on the earth.

Rose Macaulay on Dick Sheppard

23 The Vaishnava poet-saints had left an indelible mark on Gandhi's consciousness, men of humble origin whose idea of the religious life centred on a horizontal expansion of fellow-feeling, and for whom God Himself was conceived as Friend. It is largely thanks to them that Gandhi is able to envisage man's destiny as that of becoming an 'ocean of friendliness'. This is not an ocean in which individual identity is swallowed up. Friend-

ship presupposes discreteness. It also presupposes the possibility of reaching out, of forging the voluntary bonds of fellowship which, in their supreme form, are in India traditionally associated with sweetness.

Margaret Chatterjee on Mahatma Gandhi

24 From this time onward he became my friend. I knew him both in his public and in his private life; and with him, more than with most men, the link between the two was blurred. For this reason there were times when I saw more of him, knew more of the inner workings of his mind than at others. When we were ardently aligned on public issues he liked to share his thoughts with me. He poured them out in a molten torrent and we burned and glowed together in passionate agreement. But when we differed, our disagreement was all the more distasteful to him because I was his friend. He reproached me with a glowering look: 'You are not *on my side*' – and took scant interest in the reasons which had brought me to this pass. Disagreement was, in any form, obnoxious to him, but when combined with personal affection it became a kind of treachery. He demanded partisanship from a friend, at the worst, acquiescence.

Violet Bonham Carter on Winston Churchill

25 The people I love mean more to me than all the public things even if you do think that public affairs should be my chief vocation. I only do the public things because there are a few close people whom I love dearly and who matter to me above everything else. There are not so many of them and you are now one of them and I shall just have to try not to bother you so much.

Eleanor Roosevelt to Dr David Gurewitsch

26 Sometime in the early twenties he formed the most lasting friendship of his life – with Archie Lush, generally known as plain

Archie or Arch. Archie's background was the same as Anuerin's: he came from a nonconformist miner's home in Georgetown at the other end of Tredegar. When they first met, on the fringe of the crowd at some argumentative meeting in the Tredegar streets, Archie was unemployed. Suspected of having a weak heart, he never considered going down the pit and eventually got a job as an uncertified teacher at two pounds a week. He was a black-haired, irrepressible Puck, barely five feet tall, with an endless store of Welsh satire, wit, humour and relevant or irrelevant learning. At once he was captivated by Anuerin's individuality of mind, the original twist he gave to every argument, his breath-taking iconoclasm, his apparent capacity to pluck ideas out of the air like a conjuror. They had been reared on the same doctrines, and liked to look at the world with the same resolute irreverence. But Archie acknowledged his master; this new philosopher never expounded what he had learnt from others without adding his own flash of inspiration. Anuerin in turn, for the rest of his days, was always eager to test his judgments by the standards of Archie's gay wisdom. The mutual trust was absolute.

Michael Foot on Aneurin Bevan

27 He cared desperately about his friends, and the small change of social intercourse assumed an unusual importance in his life. In the midst of a period of high success he could be temporarily but deeply cast down by the unexpected failure of some small private event to which he had been looking forward. As a result, he conspicuously lacked that quality of cool, tough detachment from individual affections which is often considered essential for a leading politician. He could be blind to the faults of those whom he liked and equally blind to the virtues of those he did not – and in neither case was he in the least influenced by the calculation of who could be useful to him. He would sometimes throw away political allies with an

67

extraordinary recklessness, yet he clung to personal friendship with a persistent loyalty.

Roy Jenkins on Hugh Gaitskell

28 One of Iain Macleod's nicest attributes was his loyalty to his friends, especially if they were in trouble and needed his support. When Peter Goldman was defeated at Orpington and, later, Humphrey Berkeley at Lancaster, Iain was the first to go to them to console and sympathize. As Norman St John Stevas put it, 'Iain always forgave an injury, but he never forgot a benefit.'

Nigel Fisher on Iain Macleod

29 Friendship can overcome even the fiercest political differences . . . One cannot fail to be impressed by the story A. J. P. Taylor tells of Lord Beaverbrook. Beaverbrook had a great affection for Michael Foot who was at one time Editor of his *Evening Standard*. On one occasion after he had left the *Standard*, Michael Foot needed £3000 to prevent *Tribune*, of which paper he was the Editor, from going bankrupt. He went to Beaverbrook who immediately gave it to him. Years after Beaverbrook's death, Taylor, who was his biographer, came across details of this transaction. He telephoned Michael Foot and asked him if he wanted it put in. Michael Foot immediately agreed, and Taylor said, 'Normally of course I would put everything in, but I had to remember Max's golden rule "Nothing to ever harm Mike".' Whatever view one may take of Lord Beaverbrook, he emerges as a man who knew about the nature of true friendship.

Nadir Dinshaw on Lord Beaverbrook

30 At law as in politics, Mandela and Tambo were complementary personalities: Mandela a passionate man with a great zest for life, Tambo more reflective and deliberate. Both men were

angered by injustice, but Mandela was more assertive in expressing that anger.

'For years we worked side by side,' wrote Tambo in an introduction to a collection of Mandela's writings and speeches.

'To reach our desks each morning Nelson and I ran the gauntlet of patient queues of people overflowing from the chairs in the waiting-room into the corridors . . . We had risen to professional status in our community, but every case in court, every visit to the prisons to interview clients, reminded us of the humiliation and suffering burning into our people.'

Mary Benson on Nelson Mandela and Oliver Tambo

31 Steve was special. Being with him made a special occasion. Knowing him was an enriching experience.

He was delightful company, full of charm, large and easy and gentle and courteous and humorous. He was always completely in command, completely self-possessed – and completely unassuming. There was, of course, no need for statement or pretence, he was so obviously the real thing. He always seemed to be in buoyant spirits and lifted yours with his. He was no ascetic. He loved life and its good things and imparted this relish. But he thought that everyone should have a fair share . . .

Despite his towering stature, despite constant harrassment and frustration, he remained the most modest and most moderate and tolerant of men. After every meeting with Steve you wanted to go out and say to people: Come and meet this man. Come and talk to him, and you will find the right balance again, you will get the true perspective . . .

In a mad, confused world, he remained normal and sane and good. These were his reference points, his beacons and signposts. These, and not any imported or ready-made ideology, were his policy makers. Everyone who met Steve in good will experienced a sort of magnetism. I attribute it to his triumphant, unassailable normality, a touchstone you were welcome to share . . .

I did think of him as indestructible. As it happens I was wrong about his body. I had obviously attributed to it the same qualities as his transcendent spirit. It lives on, setting alight thousands of hearts and minds. May it purify them and strengthen them and light up the right path and lead them to the just and peaceful land he wanted with a fair share for every citizen.

Dr Trudi Thomas on Steve Biko

32   We know each other by doing so many things together, from croquet to bathing (me for the first time) in the icy moon, poetry and very high teas, getting drunk, reading, reading, reading, sea staring, Swansea, Gower, Laugharne, London . . . I've written thousands of letters to you; if you've kept some you could use what you liked to help build up this 'human portrait' of this fat pleader.

Dylan Thomas to Vernon Watkins

33   Later on, when I got to know Marlene quite well, she told me: 'I never ask Ernest for advice as such but he is always there to talk to, to get letters from, and in conversation and letters I find the things I can use for whatever problems I may have; he has often helped me without even knowing my problems. He says remarkable things that seem to automatically adjust to problems of all sizes.

For example I spoke to him on the telephone just a few weeks ago . . . he had finished writing for the day and he wanted to talk. At one point he asked me what work plans I had – if any – and I told him that I had just had a very lucrative offer from a Miami nightclub but I was undecided about whether to take it.

"Why the indecision?" he asked.

"Well," I answered, "I feel I should work. I should not waste my time. It's wrong. I think one appearance in London and one a year in Vegas is quite enough. However I'm probably just pampering myself, so I've been trying to convince myself to take the offer."

There was silence for a moment and I could visualize Ernest's beautiful face poised in thought. He finally said, "Don't do what you don't sincerely want to do. Never confuse movement with action."

In those five words he gave me a whole philosophy. That's the wonderful thing about him – he kneels himself into his friend's problems. He is like a huge rock off somewhere, a constant and steady thing, that certain someone whom everybody should have and nobody has.'

A. E. Hotchner on Marlene Dietrich and Ernest Hemingway

34   Although I knew Joyce when I was five, we did not become staunch and everlasting friends until we were in our early teens, when we found each other irresistibly funny, so wildly entertaining, we formed a sort of mutual admiration society that continued, I am proud to say, until she died. We also shared an unorthodox religion, Christian Science, which in those unecumenical days entailed a certain amount of gentle persecution. And we ate our baked beans on toast at Lyons Corner House before going to a matinee – and we did this every week, though sometimes to be dashing we changed to Welsh rarebit – and we would air our doubts and convictions, nodding wisely like very old owls, as we pondered on the Creation, or, later in the meal, between sucks at our strawberry nut sundaes, on Eternity . . . As a friend her main virtue – and she had many subsidiary ones – was her reliability. She was not mercurial; whatever the temperature, she did not change. She was as steady, and come hell or high water, as comforting as a nanny, and like that moribund figure there was not an ounce of malice in her. There were times, certainly in her professional life, when she was badly treated, but she seemed incapable of being angry or bearing ill-will. She could admonish, and frequently did so; the queue jumper and the theatre chatterer getting their ears

71

gently knocked back, much to their surprise; but it was in a reformatory rather than an exasperated style.

Virginia Graham on Joyce Grenfell

35   C. S. Lewis' account of how true friendship begins when two acquaintances discover that they have some common insight or taste recalls his and Tolkein's discovery of their mutual delight in 'Northernness'. His assertion that friendship thrives not so much on agreeing about the answers as on agreeing what are the important questions reminds one of the way in which he and Barfield continued on close terms long after they had disagreed on fundamental religious issues. His assertion that friendship is not inquisitive – 'You can become a man's friend without knowing or caring whether he is married or single or how he earns his living' – is a statement of his own obstinate refusal to admit private matters into conversation with his friends. And his declaration that real friendship is not jealous, and that 'in each of my friends there is something that only some other friend can fully bring out' perhaps comes closest of all to explaining what the Inklings were fundamentally about.

Humphrey Carpenter on The Inklings

36   On what would have been Dame Gladys Cooper's eighty-second birthday, Patricia and I took Sybil, now in her ninetieth year, once more to the 'Actor's Church' for the thanksgiving service for Gladys' life. It was a happy service with everyone feeling that Gladys was present, delighted to see all her friends, all the actors and actresses. When it was over, we put Sybil in the car, but couldn't get away because of the crowd. So we opened the window of the car and Sybil, as it were, held court sitting in the car in the churchyard. She saw all her friends and Gladys' friends and was enchanted. As we finally drove out she turned to us and said, 'What a lovely party! And how much Gladys must have enjoyed it. When's the next Memorial Service?'

John Casson on Sybil Thorndike

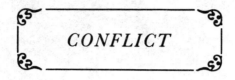

CONFLICT

1   With every true friendship we build more firmly the foundations
     on which the peace of the whole world rests.

     Mahatma Gandhi

2   In old days those who went to fight
          In three days had one year's leave.
          But in *this* war the soldiers are never changed;
          They must go on fighting until they die on the battlefield.
          I thought of you, so weak and indolent.
          Hopelessly trying to learn to march and drill.
          That a young man should ever come home again
          Seemed about as unlikely as that the sky should fall.
          Since I got the news that you were coming back,
          Twice I have mounted to the high wall of your home.
          I found your brother mending your horse's stall;
          I found your mother sewing your new clothes.
          I am half afraid; perhaps it is not true;
          Yet I never weary of watching for you on the road.
          Each day I go out to the City Gate
          With a flask of wine, lest you should come thirsty.
          Oh that I could shrink the surface of the world,
          So that suddenly I might find you standing at my side!

          Wang-Chien

3   I am well aware of the obloquy people have heaped upon me
     since the death of Caesar. They put it down to my discredit that
     I am sorely grieved at the death of a very intimate friend and
     resent the fall of one I loved; for they declare that patriotism
     must come before friendship, just as if they had already
     demonstrated that his death had been to the benefit of the State.

But I shall use no ingenuous arguments; I frankly confess I have not reached that high level of philosophy.

Cicero

4   *More* Howard, you must cease to know me.

Norfolk I do know you! I wish I didn't but I do!

More I mean as a friend.

Norfolk You *are* my friend!

More I can't relieve you of your obedience to the King, Howard. You must relieve yourself of our friendship. No one's safe now, and you have a son.

Norfolk You might as well advise a man to change the colour of his hair! I'm fond of you and there it is! You're fond of me and there it is!

More What's to be done then?

Norfolk (with deep appeal) Give in.

More (gently) I can't give in, Howard (smile) – you might as well advise a man to change the colour of his eyes. I can't. Our friendship is more mutable than *that*.

Norfolk Oh, that's immutable is it? The one fixed point in a world of changing friendships is that Thomas More will not give in!

More (urgent to explain) To me it *has* to be, for that's myself! Affection goes as deep in me as you think, but only God is love right through, Howard, and that's myself!

Robert Bolt

5   Even before coming to America, William Penn wrote the Indians concerning his colony, 'I desire to enjoy it with your consent, that we may always live together as neighbours and friends', and he promised to 'live justly, peaceably and friendly' with them. On reaching America, unlike most other colonists, Penn paid the Indians for the land before, not after the settlers had moved in . . . Against the 'prayerful and considered' advice of other colonists, Penn and his followers went unarmed. The

76

Pennsylvanians and the Indians visited one another's houses and wigwams . . . and for seventy years lived in peace and mutual security.

When, in 1756, the Pennsylvania Council, no longer under Quaker control, declared war on the Indians, Friends withdrew from the provincial government for two reasons: they did not believe in war; they still believed in their policy of non-violence and respect for the Indians. They opposed the war, refused to pay taxes for its support and formed the 'Friendly Association for Gaining and Preserving Peace with the Indians by Pacific Measures'. In 1758, at the cost of £5000 voluntarily subscribed, the Association achieved its end and peace was restored.

American Quaker Report

6   The day came finally for Lincoln to select a man to fill the all-important post of Secretary of War. Can you imagine who Lincoln chose to fill this post? None other than the man named Stanton. There was an immediate uproar in the inner circle when the news began to spread. Adviser after adviser was heard saying, 'Mr President, you are making a mistake. Do you know this man Stanton? . . .' Mr Lincoln's answer was terse and to the point: 'Yes, I know Mr Stanton. I am aware of all the terrible things he has said about me. But after looking over the nation, I find he is the best man for the job.'

If Lincoln had hated Stanton both men would have gone to their graves as bitter enemies. But through the power of love Lincoln transformed an enemy into a friend. It was this same attitude that made it possible for Lincoln to speak a kind word about the South during the Civil War when feeling was most bitter. Asked by a shocked bystander how he could do this, Lincoln said, 'Madam, do I not destroy my enemies when I make them my friends?'

Martin Luther King

7   Love is a rare herb that makes a friend even of a sworn enemy and this herb grows out of non-violence . . . It is the acid test of non-violence that there is no rancour left behind and, in the end, the enemies are converted into friends. That was my experience in South Africa with General Smuts. He started with being my bitterest opponent and critic. Today he is my warmest friend.

Mahatma Gandhi

8   I walked around the company as often as I could. Whenever men were hit they invariably sent for me, because they wanted to shake hands before either they died or went wounded to the dressing station. Their eyes were eloquent. Although they might not be able to speak or find words there was sometimes a quality in their gaze suggesting that they were giving thanks for past favours and friendship and expressing regret that the end of our comradeship had come, the future totally unknown. I remember especially a splendid corporal with whom I had developed a special rapport in the course of long months of working together. He could hardly speak but he took both my hands in his, looking into my eyes and talking to me with his eyes while awaiting the arrival of the stretcher.

In retrospect I can only think of David's superb lament over the death of Saul and Jonathan. Paraphrasing the Bible account, it might be said that in one of the fiercest battles in modern history he had been slain in a high place and that one of the mighty had fallen. He was lovely and pleasant in his life.

Henry Lawson

9   The men floating in this ark were detached and their thoughts could wander unfettered. They were not hungry and not full. They were not happy and therefore not disturbed by the prospect of forfeiting happiness. Their heads were not full of trivial worries about their jobs, office intrigue or anxieties about promotion, their shoulders unbowed by cares about housing, fuel, food and clothing for their children. Love, man's age-old

source of pleasure and suffering, was powerless to touch them, either its agony or its expectation. Their terms of imprisonment were so long that none of them had started to think of the time when they would be released. Men of outstanding intellect, education and experience, who were normally too devoted to their families to have enough of themselves to spare for friendship, were here wholly given over to their friends. From this ark, serenely ploughing its ways through the darkness, it was easy for them to survey, as from a great height, the whole tortuous, errant flow of history; yet at the same time, like people completely immersed in it, they could see every pebble in its depths.

On these Sunday evenings the physical, material world never intruded. A spirit of manly friendship and philosophy hovered over the sail-shaped vault of the ceiling. Was this, perhaps, that state of bliss which all the philosophers of antiquity tried in vain to define and describe?

Alexander Solzhenitsyn

10 When he died (in Czechoslovakia) in 1952 Karol Smidke was in even greater official disfavour than when Siroky had initially condemned him . . . No one in the Party wanted to have anything to do with him, and no one was willing to speak at his funeral. All the top leaders made some sort of excuse and not one of them was prepared to taint his own reputation by association with the name or even with the grave of Smidke. Dubcek was appalled that this great, loyal and well-loved man should be denied any recognition and, when everyone else refused to attend the funeral, he accepted. So it happened that at Smidke's death his life was lauded only by this very junior and insignificant bureaucrat.

There were only about fifty people at the cold and windy burial service; most of them from Smidke's family and several others were STB men taking photographs and names. Apart from Dubcek there were only three Party officials there.

Dubcek's speech was courageous. He heaped praise upon the outlawed and disgraced leader. 'Smidke,' he said, 'was a great member of the Party, a true revolutionary who gave his whole self and his every effort for the battle for which our Party has fought.' Dubcek was weeping as he finished his address.

William Shawcross

11 . . . Nothing ever affected me as deeply as President Kennedy's death, not even the news that Martin had been stabbed in Harlem. Because John Kennedy had been so kind and thoughtful to us, we felt that he was a friend to be relied upon, as well as our President. Our family shared that feeling, and when the children came home from school that afternoon, Yoki came flying up the stairs wailing, 'Mommy! Mommy!' Daddy King was going downstairs, and as he passed her, he asked in a troubled tone, 'What's the matter, Yoki?'

She did not stop to answer, but kept on running to me. She said, 'Mommy, they've killed President Kennedy, and he didn't do one single thing to anybody.' And then Yoki added, 'Oh Mommy, we're never going to get our freedom now.'

Watching Jacqueline Kennedy, who was so courageous in her tragedy, and watching her small children, I could not help thinking about my husband, especially because so many people considered Martin's work more dangerous even than the President's. It was as if, watching the funeral, I was steeling myself for our own fate.

Martin and I, for all our philosophical explanations and our deep faith in God, were still personally in the dark abyss of sorrow for this gallant, compassionate and wise young man – a true statesman. On that sombre day, little Marty, who was six, said to his father, 'Daddy, President Kennedy was your best friend, wasn't he, Daddy?'

In a way he was.

Coretta Scott King

12   . . . And you
my friends
my allies
cosily chaired in London
or termiting in a thousand towns
or treadmilling the arid round
of priest, picket, pamphlet –
for as long as fervour lasts:
what shall I say of us?

O let Chief's reflected splendour
and the aura resistance sometimes brings –
except to the jaded, jaundiced, cynic –
O let us catch a little of this fire
and let us burn and steadily assert
our faith, our will to freedom and our love
for freedom and our dear unhappy land:
of inexhaustible and hungry fire
of love and hunger and imperishable resolve.

And the men
the dear lonely men
gaunt, and with a hunger round their eyes,
and the busy women
friendly strangers in a hundred lands:
ah these my comrades and my friends!
How long, oh how much longer must it be?
how long still the wrench of the throat
the pluck at eyes
at mention of some forgotten word –
Fietas or Woodstock or Gelvendale? –
how much longer must we doggedly importune
in the anterooms of governors of the world
or huddle stubborn on the draughty frontiers
    of strange lands?
how long must we endure?
and how shall I express my gratitude and love?

   Dennis Brutus

13 You were my friend
    When I fought my liberation war,
    You gave me shelter
    From the enemy's striking power.

    You were the base
    From which I launched my campaign,
    You were a buffer
    'Twixt me and the battle-line.

    You were my cushion
    To absorb the shock of combat casualties,
    You were the mirror
    Reflecting images of glory and freedom.

    You boosted my morale
    When I'd been way down under,
    You sang a song
    Of the people's day of victory.

    Life joys we shared
    Of battles won across the borders,
    Death fire we shared
    When enemy fury poured from the sky.

    You were at my side
    When the people's victory was won.
    Remain my friend,
    My good neighbour, Frontline State.

Canaan Banana

14 Colour meant nothing. Anyone
    who wanted help, had humour or was kind
    was brother to you; categories of skin
    were foreign; you were colour-blind.

And then the revolution. Black
and loud the horns of anger blew
against the long oppression; sufferers
cast off the precious value of the few.

New powers re-enslaved us all:
each person manacled in skin, in race.
You could not wear your paid-up dues;
the keen discriminators typed your face.

The future darkening, you thought it time
to say good-bye. It may be you were right.
It hurt to see you go; but, more,
it hurt to see you slowly going white.

Mervyn Morris

15   By the rivers of foreign countries we sat down
        as refugees;
there we wept when we remembered the land
    of our birth.
We stopped singing our beloved songs
    of liberation.
Those who are helping our enemies wanted to sing;
    they wanted us to entertain them:
'Sing us a song about the land whence you fled.'

How can they expect us to entertain them
    with our suffering and tears?
May I never turn our struggle for freedom and peace
    into entertainment for those who are
    friends of our enemies!
May I never be able to sing again
    if I do not remember you,
    if I do not think of you,
    O country of my birth!

Zephania Kameeta

16   Because we feel that you are among us
In each flower, at each corner,
On our silent march;
Because one day you wept beside me
And wiped away my tears;
Because you had faith in this struggle
With only your ardour to guide you;
Because you never doubted
That one day truth will triumph;
Because your voice was always alert
For the one whose spirit was flagging;
Because your example blazed the trail for us,
And because of so much more, my sister,
We draw from your strength
Courage and hope.

And that is why it does not seem
Such an absurd idea to me
That we shall find you among us,
One day, in our Square.

C. Adel

17 We have to talk over with you, God
What we'll need for peace –
We'll need a lot more friends
If we're going to make more peace –
Friends from different classes
Friends from different churches
Friends with different interests, even if we don't like them
Friends who share a vision of peace and justice that can be
    achieved.

Dorothee Sölle

Sometimes I wish
My eyes hadn't been opened,
Sometimes I wish
I could no longer see
All of the pain
And the hurt and the longing
Of my sisters and me
As we try to be free.

Sometimes I wish
My eyes hadn't been opened,
Just for an hour
How sweet it would be
Not to be struggling,
Not to be striving,
But just sleep securely
In our slavery.

But now that I've seen
With my eyes, I can't close them.
Because deep inside me
Somewhere I'd know
The road that my sisters and I have to travel:
My heart would say 'Yes'
And my feet would say 'Go!'

Sometimes I wish
My eyes hadn't been opened,
But now that they have
I'm determined to see
That somehow my sisters
And I will be one day
The free people we were
Created to be.

Carole Etzler

19 To be persons, in the Christian sense, means that we must bear one another's burdens. We must be prepared to suffer pain for one another and to carry each other in love through times of darkness and dread. We must take on what we can of each other's violence and woundedness without allowing ourselves the relief of retaliation. Only if we are prepared to do this do we enter the privilege of the gospel, which is to heal each other and find our healing in and through each other.

Angela Tilby

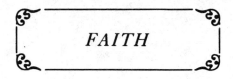

FAITH

1　God is Friendship

　　Aelred of Rievaulx

2　Within your beautiful works I see Him, the All-Beautiful . . .
He who can remind us of God, he alone is the true friend.

　　Sarojimi Chourdney to C. F. Andrews

3　Lovers are the children of Nature; Friends the children of God.

　　Henry Thoreau

4　It's impossible to love anybody without loving God.

　　Max Plowman

5　Abraham believed God and it was imputed unto him for
righteousness and he was called the Friend of God.

　　James 2.23

6　And the Lord spake unto Moses face to face as a man speaketh
unto his friend.

　　Exodus 33.11

7　And it came to pass, when he had made an end of speaking unto
Saul that the soul of Jonathan was knit with the soul of David
and Jonathan loved him as his own soul.

　　1 Samuel 18.1

8　Ruth said, 'Entreat me not to leave thee, or to return from
following after thee: for whither thou goest, I will go; and where

thou lodgest I will lodge; thy people shall be my people, and thy God my God: where thou diest, will I die, and there will I be buried: the Lord do so to me, and more also if ought but death part thee and me.'

Ruth 1.16–19

9 Ointment and perfume rejoice the heart: so doth the sweetness of a man's friend by hearty counsel.

Thine own friend, and thy father's friend, forsake not; neither go into thy brother's house in the day of thy calamity; for better is a neighbour that is near than a brother far off.

Proverbs 27.9–10

10 Pleasant words win many friends, and an affable manner makes acquaintance easy. Accept a greeting from everyone, but advice from only one in a thousand. When you make a friend, begin by testing him, and be in no hurry to trust him. Some friends are loyal when it suits them but desert you in time of trouble. Some friends turn into enemies and shame you by making the quarrel public. Another sits at your table but is nowhere to be found in time of trouble. Hold your enemies at a distance, and keep a wary eye on your friends. A faithful friend is a secure shelter; whoever finds one has found a treasure. A faithful friend is beyond price; his worth is more than money can buy. A faithful friend is an elixir of life, found only by those who fear the Lord. The man who fears the Lord keeps his friendships in repair, for he treats his neighbour as himself.

Ecclesiasticus 6.6–17

11 Do not desert an old friend; a new one is not worth as much. A new friend is like new wine; you do not enjoy drinking it until it has matured.

Ecclesiasticus 9.10

12 Greater love hath no man than this, that a man lay down his life for his friends.

Ye are my friends, if ye do whatsoever I command you.

Henceforth I call you not servants, for the servant knoweth not what his lord doeth; but I have called you friends; for all things that I have heard of my Father I have made known unto you.

John 15.13–14

13 We have already noted that, to the infinite scandal of all respectable people, Jesus chose his friends among the poor, the alienated, the underprivileged and the socially discarded. It was taken for granted that a religious teacher would move in the society of the virtuous, the polished and the well-to-do and that he would become interested in the others only when they had reached a certain stage in the transformation of themselves into respectability. Jesus swept away all such prudential ideas with the one trenchant maxim, 'They that are whole have no need of a physician, but they that are sick.' He seems really to have liked his disreputable friends and to have found among them a sincerity and an openness to the realities of life that are often lacking among those whose existence has been cushioned against those harsh realities. He was prepared to accept them in their pathetic absurdity, their alienation from society, and the darkening of their minds and spirits. They could not wear out his patience; stupid, inconstant and faithless; they found him changeless and always the same. He was prepared to trust them even when they were not worthy of any trust.

Stephen Neill

14 We saw how Jesus, out of that joy in God called by the old word 'gospel', became a friend. His celebration was not only the 'wedding of the soul with God', as the old hymn has it, but 'the feast of heaven and earth', namely the celebration of that coming Kingdom which will restore heaven and earth. This

celebration makes friends and brings friendships to light everywhere. As it seems to a child, a friend is someone who likes you. It can be absolutely anyone and anything in the world that can accept you as you are.

Jürgen Moltmann

15 The disciples at Emmaus, we are told, knew him in the breaking of bread. It is the symbol of hospitality, of friendship. And we, if we are to live consciously in his companionship, must give him the marks of our friendship in our turn. Now I call you not servants but friends, he explicitly told his disciples; we have only to do our part . . . not just a sharing of superficialities such as exists between acquaintances, but a sharing of the deep things of life, the deep thoughts and ambitions, the secrets of the heart. Our Lord, for his part, calls us not servants but friends, because, he says, he has made known to us the secrets of his own heart, has shown us the plot of his own love-story: it only remains for us to do the same.

Gerald Vann

16 I find it hard to believe that Our Lord after he had washed the disciples' feet said, 'If I then, your Lord and Master, have washed your feet, ye ought also to wash one another's feet.' It is difficult to reconcile these words with the words he had just used to St Peter, 'What I do thou knowest not now; but thou shalt know hereafter.' The feet-washing seems to me a much more spontaneous act of love and affection carried over into a dramatic and ritual act than an object lesson in Christian service. As a spontaneous act of friendship it embodies the true relation between friendship and saintliness. There is about it both solemnity and naturalness, both holiness and the human joy of touching and tending the bodies of those we love. Take away from the whole story any suggestion that it was in any sense an object lesson to his disciples. See it rather as something complete, natural and fitting in itself, whose full value began

and ended with its performance. It then takes on for us, for whose sake it is reported, a new value of its own. It comes to us not as a lesson as to how we should act, but as a picture of Our Lord's way of living with others in a way in which saintliness and friendship are blended without self-consciousness or strain.

R. O. Hall

17 When we look at the model of Jesus' ministry in the Gospels, it is a model that we would do well to copy in our contemporary society, the model of growing groups of friends . . . Jesus as friend and brother was an important ingredient within that group. Jesus is known to countless disciples under various models. He is known as a Saviour, as Redeemer, as Lord, as Master; but he is no less friend and brother. The prayer of St Richard of Chichester has about it a contemporary ring:

O Holy Jesus, most merciful Redeemer, our Friend and our Brother, may we know you more clearly, love you more dearly, and follow you more nearly day by day.

Indeed it was this prayer which was made popular for thousands and thousands of people outside the life of the Church through that vibrant presentation of the musical 'Godspell'. 'Godspell' was a presentation of the theme of friendship with Jesus, the friend in the midst.

Ivor Smith-Cameron

18   What do I have, that you seek out my friendship?
    What can there be leading you, my Jesus,
    Through the wintry nights of darkness,
    Drenched with dew, here beside my door?

    O what hardness must I have within me,
    Not to let you in! What strange perversity,
    If with the icy cold of my ingratitude
    The open wounds of your pure feet were dried!

How many times have I heard the angel tell me:
'Souls, glimpse now at the window;
See with how much love he insistent calls!'

And how many times, sweet Sovereign,
Have I answered, 'Tomorrow shall let him in . . .'
Merely upon the morrow to answer thus again!

Lope de Vega

19 So that to your question, how far a dear and perfect friendship is
authorized by the principles of Christianity? The answer is
ready and easy. It is warranted to extend to all mankind; and
the more we love, the better we are and the greater our
friendships are, and the nearer we are to God; let them be as
dear and let them be as perfect, and let them be as many as you
can; there is no danger in it; only where the restraint begins,
there begins our imperfection; it is not ill that you entertain
brave friendships and worthy societies; it were well if you could
love and if you could *benefit* all mankind; for I conceive that is the
sum of all friendships.

Jeremy Taylor

20 Otherwise, be persuaded on the word of others, while waiting
for experience to make you taste and feel, that this detachment
from self and from all that you love, far from withering good
friendships and hardening your heart, produces, on the contrary, a friendship in God, not only pure and firm, but
completely cordial, faithful, affectionate, full of sweet relationship. And we find that all the fullness of friendship which
human nature seeks for its consolation.

François Fénelon

21 In prayer we all find each other; we can all meet each other in
God. Either the personality of the other person is surrendered to
the Eternal and we love him, he is our friend, because we love

what he is rooted in. Or else the other person is not grounded and rooted and living in the Eternal, and then he is an unhappy creature to whom everything must be forgiven and whom we must love all the more to turn him into a friend.

I am not in the least mad – I am free, that is normal; free of you too, my friends, if God requires it; but in going God's way, I shall return to you at a deeper level . . . free of you, my friend, the better to belong to you, to be with you . . . The essential 'We', instead of the illusory 'I'.

Pierre Ceresole

22　Request and answer are the two sides of friendship with God. And friendship with God gives prayer the certainty that it will be answered . . . Prayer and answer are what constitute human friendship with God and divine friendship with human beings. It seems to me important to place both the praying and the answering on the plane of friendship. For then it is a relation of mutual affection and of respect for freedom. A friend asks out of affection; but at the same time respects the other's freedom . . . Prayer in Christ's name is the language of friendship.

Jürgen Moltmann

23　When we are drowned in the overwhelming seas of the love of God, we find ourselves in a new and particular relation to a few of our fellows. The relation is so surprising and so rich that we despair of finding a word glorious enough and weighty enough to name it. The word *fellowship* is discovered, but the word is pale and thin in comparison with the rich volume and luminous bulk and warmth of the experience which it would designate. For a new kind of life-sharing and of love has arisen of which we had only dim hints before. Are these the bonds which knit together the early Christians, the very warp and woof of the Kingdom of God?

Thomas Kelly

24 I thank my God upon every remembrance of you, always in every prayer of mine for you all making request with joy, for your fellowship in the gospel from the first day until now.

Philippians 1.3–4

25   Why hast thou cast our lot
        In the same age and place,
      And why together brought
        To see each other's face,
      To join with loving sympathy,
      And mix our friendly souls in Thee?

      Didst thou not make us one,
        That we might one remain,
      Together travel on,
        And share our joy and pain,
      Till all thy utmost goodness prove,
      And rise renewed in perfect love?

Charles Wesley

26 The Church is not meant to be filled with a bunch of self-confident success types; it is composed of people who know that without God's help they are no good to man or beast, and it is surprising, when you get to know them from inside, as I do, how different they look. They may look dull and uninspiring to the outward eye, but sometimes a God's-eye-view of them has come my way, and has shown them to be what they really are: a bunch of ordinary human beings which, relying on God, is full of many mini-Mother Teresas and pocket Wesleys and Wilberforces in tired and dilapidated cassocks doing their best to love God and their fellows; and at such times, I wouldn't swop them for any other bunch of people in God's world.

Anthony Bridge

27   My own experience was always of warm and real friendships in religious life. My school days' sense that the nuns were women of wholeness as well as holiness was not disappointed in the reality of community. At one time I would have said that all women were meant to be mothers, and that nuns were not exempt from this . . . But a fellow religious disagreed with me and said that women were meant to be those who loved and were prepared to be loved, and that it was in this that fullness of humanity came. She was right, and it is both women and men of whom this is true. Wholeness will come only to those who love; and love, of course, is lived in relationship whatever the context of a chosen way of life.

Prue Wilson

28   If anyone were to ask me, 'What's the most important thing in life for you?' I think I would probably have to answer in a single word, 'Friends'. Of course some friends are more important than others; but quite a number are very important to me. And if someone were to say to me, 'But as a priest, isn't God more important to you than any of your friends?' I'd have to say that God is above all and through all and in all; and it's in and through my friends that I think I have learnt, and still do learn, most about God and receive most from Him.

Eric James

29   'The diffrense from a person and an angel is easy. Most of an angel is in the inside and most of a person is on the outside.' These are the words of six-year-old Anna, sometimes called Mouse, Hum or Joy. At five years Anna knew absolutely the purpose of being, knew the meaning of love and was a personal friend and helper of Mister God. At six Anna was a theologian, mathematician, philosopher, poet and gardener. If you asked her a question you would always get an answer – in due course. On some occasions the answer would be delayed for weeks or months; but eventually, in her own good time, the answer would come: direct, simple and much to the point.

She never made eight years, she died by an accident. She died with a grin on her beautiful face. She died saying, 'I bet Mister God lets me get into heaven for this,' and I bet he did too.

Fynn

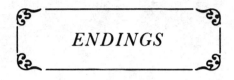

ENDINGS

1   Saul and Jonathan were lovely and pleasant in their lives,
And in their death they were not divided.

    I Samuel 1.20

2   For my own part, I am transported with impatience to join the
society of my departed friends, and to be with mighty men of the
past of whom I have read. To this glorious assembly I am
quickly advancing; and if some divinity should offer me life over
again I would reject the offer. This world is a place which
Nature never designed for my permanent abode; and I look
upon my departure, not as being driven from my home, but as
leaving my inn.

    Cicero

3   What have we done to you, death
that you treat us so,
with always another catch
one day a warrior
the next a head of state;
charmed by the loyal
you choose the best.
Iniquitous, unequalling death
I would not complain
if you were just
but you take the worthy
leaving fools for us.

Fifty years among us
upholding rights
annulling wrongs,
impatient death

could you not wait
a little longer?
He still would be here
and mine, a brother
without a flaw. Peace
be upon him and Spring
rains water his tomb but
could you not wait
a little longer?
You came too soon.

Al-Khansa (?)

4 Blue hills over the north wall;
White water swirling to the east of the city:
This is where you must leave me –
A long puff of thistledown
 on a thousand mile journey.
Ah the drifting clouds
 and the thoughts of a wanderer!
The setting sun
 and emotions of old friends.
A wave of the hand now
 and you are gone.
Our horses whinnied to each other at parting.

Li Po

5 When to the sessions of sweet silent thought
I summon up remembrance of things past,
I sigh the lack of many a thing I sought,
And with old woes new wail my dear times' waste;
Then can I drown an eye, unused to flow,
For precious friends hid in death's dateless night,
And weep afresh love's long-since-cancelled woe,
And moan the expense of many a vanished sight.
Then can I grieve at grievances foregone

And heavily from woe to woe tell o'er
The sad account of fore-bemoaned moan,
Which I new pay as if not paid before.
But if the while I think on thee, dear Friend,
All losses are restored, and sorrows end.

William Shakespeare

6 After this it was noised abroad that Mr Valiant was taken with a
summons by the same post as the other; and he called for his
friends and told them of it. Then said he, 'I am going to my
Father's; and though with great difficulty I am got hither, yet
now I do not repent me of all the trouble I have been at to arrive
where I am. My sword I give to him that shall succeed me in my
pilgrimage, and my courage and skill to him that can get it. My
marks and scars I carry with me, to be a witness for me that I
have fought His battles who now will be my rewarder.'

When the day that he must go hence was come many
accompanied him to the riverside, into which as he went he
said, 'Death, where is thy sting?' And as he went down deeper
he said 'Grave, where is thy victory?' So he passed over, and all
the trumpets sounded for him on the other side.

John Bunyan

7 They are all gone into the world of light!
    And I alone sit lingering here;
Their very memory is fair and bright,
    And my sad thoughts doth clear.

It glows and glitters in my cloudy breast
    Like stars upon some gloomy grove,
Or those faint beams in which this hill is dressed,
    After the sun's remove.

I see them walking in an air of glory,
    Whose light doth trample on my days:
My days which are at best but dull and hoary,
    Mere glimmering and decays.

O holy Hope! and high humility,
  High as the Heavens above!
These are your walks, and you have showed them me
  To kindle my cold love.

Dear, beauteous death! the jewel of the just,
  Shining nowhere, but in the dark;
What mysteries do lie beyond thy dust;
  Could man outlook that mark! . . .

Henry Vaughan

8   They that love beyond the world cannot be separated by it.
Death cannot kill what never dies.
Nor can spirits ever be divided that love and live in the same
    divine principle, the root and record of their friendship.
If absence be not death, neither is theirs.
Death is but the crossing the world as friends do cross the seas:
    they live in one another still.
For they must needs be present, that love and live in that which
    is omnipresent.
This is the comfort of friends, that though they may be said to
    die, yet their friendship and society are ever present, because
    immortal.

William Penn

9   Come, let us join our friends above
             That have obtained the prize,
             And on the eagle wings of love
             To joys celestial rise.
             Let all the saints terrestrial sing
             With those to glory gone.
             For all the servants of our King
             In earth and heaven are one.

Ten thousand to their endless home
This solemn moment fly;
And we are to the margin come,
And we expect to die;
Ev'n now by faith we join our hands
With those that went before,
And greet the blood-besprinkled bands
On the eternal shore.

Charles Wesley

10   Calm on the bosom of thy God,
Fair spirit, rest thee now!
E'en while with ours thy footsteps trod,
His seal was on thy brow,

Dust, to its narrow house beneath!
Soul, to its place on high!
They that have seen thy look in death
No more may fear to die.

Felicia Dorothea Hemans

11   My boat is on the shore,
And my bark is on the sea;
But, before I go, Tom Moore,
Here's a double health to thee!

Here's a sigh to those who love me,
And a smile to those who hate;
And, whatever sky's above me,
Here's a heart for every fate.

Though the ocean roar around me,
Yet it still shall bear me on;
Though a desert should surround me
It hath springs that may be won.

Were't the last drop in the well,
As I gasp'd upon the brink,
E'er my fainting spirit fell,
'Tis to thee that I would drink.

With that water, as this wine,
The libation I would pour
Should be – peace with thine and mine,
And a health to thee, Tom Moore.

Lord Byron

12
Fame is a fruit that dead men eat
I have no stomach for such meat.
In little night and narrow room,
They eat it in the silent tomb,
With no kind voice of comrade near
To bid the feaster be of cheer.

But friendship is a noble thing –
Of friendship it is good to sing
For truly, when a man shall end,
He lives in memory of his friend,
Who does his better part recall
And of his fault make funeral.

Henry Austin Dobson

13
Break, break, break,
On thy cold grey stones, O Sea!
And I would that my tongue could utter
The thoughts that arise in me.

O well for the fisherman's boy,
That he shouts with his sister at play!
O well for the sailor lad,
That he sings in his boat on the bay!

And the stately ships go on
   To their haven under the hill;
But O for the touch of a vanish'd hand,
   And the sound of a voice that is still!

Break, break, break,
   At the foot of thy crags, O Sea!
But the tender grace of a day that is dead
   Will never come back to me.

Alfred, Lord Tennyson

14

I wish that when you died last May,
Charles, there had died along with you
Three parts of Spring's delightful things;
Ay, and for me, the fourth part too.

A foolish thought, and worse, perhaps!
There must be many a pair of friends
Who, arm in arm, deserve the warm
Moon-births and the long evening-ends.

So, for their sakes, be May still May!
Let their new time, as mine of old,
Do all it did for me: I bid
Sweet sights and sounds throng manifold.

Only, one little sigh, one plant,
Woods have in May, that starts up green
Save a sole streak, which so to speak,
Is spring's blood, spilt on its leaves between, –

That, they might spare: a certain wood
Might miss the plant; their loss were small.
But I, – whene'er the leaf grows there,
Its drop comes from my heart, that's all.

Robert Browning

15   They told me, Heraclitus, they told me you were dead,
They brought me bitter news to hear and bitter tears to shed.
I wept as I remember'd how often you and I
Had tired the sun with talking and sent him down the sky.

And now that thou art lying, my dear old Carian guest,
A handful of grey ashes, long, long ago at rest,
Still are thy pleasant voices, thy nightingales, awake;
For Death, he taketh all away, but them he cannot take.

William Cory

16   Shake hands, we shall never be friends, all's over,
I only vex you the more I try.
All's wrong that ever I've done or said,
And naught to help it in this dull head:
Shake hands, here's luck, good-bye.

But if you come to a road where danger
Or guilt or anguish or shame's to share,
Do good to the lad that loves you true
And the soul that was born to die for you,
And whistle and I'll be there.

A. E. Housman

17   The sky widens to Cornwall. A sense of sea
Hangs in the lichenous branches and still there's light.
The road from its tunnel of blackthorn rises free
                To a final height.

And over the west is glowing a mackrel sky
Whose opal fleece has faded to purple pink.
In this hour of the late-lit, listening evening, why
                Do my spirits sink?

The tide is high and a sleepy Atlantic sends
Exploring ripple on ripple down Polzeath shore,

And the gathering dark is full of the thought of friends
        I shall see no more.

Where is Anne Channel who loved this place the best,
With her tense blue eyes and her shopping-bag falling apart,
And her racy gossip and a nineteen-twenty zest,
        And that warmth of heart?

Where's Roland, easing his most unwieldy car,
With its load of golf clubs, backwards into the lane?
Where Kathleen Stokes with her sealyhams? There's
  Doom's Bar;
        Bray Hill shows plain.

For this is the turn, and the well-known trees draw near;
On the road their pattern in moonlight fades and swells:
As the engine stops, from two miles off I hear
        St Minver bells.

With a host of stars in a wideness still and deep:
What a host of souls as a motor-bike whines away
And the silver snake of the estuary curls to sleep
        In Daymer Bay.

Are they one with the Celtic saints and the years between?
Can they see the moonlit pools where ribbon weed drifts?
As I reach our hill, I am part of a sea unseen –
        The oppression lifts.

   John Betjeman

18   Today I feel lost
                   amidst my birthday celebrations,
                   I wish for those friends,
                   through the touch of whose hands
                   I could take with me
                   this life's supreme grace,
                   received through the flavour
                   of pleasing communion –

                            109

the best that this earth offers –
take with me man's final blessing.
Today my bag holds nothing,
I have emptied it,
given away whatever I have to give.
If I receive something in return –
some affection – some forgiveness –
I shall have that to take with me
as I take the ferry to the other side
to join in the ultimate celebration
beyond language.

Rabindranath Tagore

19 I met him sailing at the Yellow Sea,
Sailing paper-boats, playing with tea.
He told me all the world was in his eyes,
All the souls were sodden leaves:
I looked at his eyes when he turned his cup,
And saw a few aloof in a short limpid life.

Now I hear he died in a mountain rain,
I saw the Yellow Sea he will not see again.

Awang Kedua

20 In my arms he died, that comrade tried,
His like I shall ne'er possess,
His nerves were steel and his heart was gold,
He was true and steady and wise and bold,
To pay a debt to a savage foe
He died in the wilderness.

On the sun-baked plain I dug his grave,
With my hands I heaped the sod,
My heart was full to the bitter brim,
The soil was wet where I buried him
As I knelt by the head of his narrow bed
And prayed for his soul to God.

No rite or office I left undone
Though my soul was sick with loss;
With trembling hands I cut two sticks,
And as best I could, made a crucifix;
And there in the wild I left my friend
Asleep 'neath that little cross . . .

José Hernández

21

It was beautiful
As long as it lasted
The journey of my life.

I have no regrets
Whatsoever save
The pain I'll leave behind.

Those dear hearts
Who love and care
And the heavy with sleep
Ever moist eyes
The smile in spite of a
Lump in the throat
And the strings pulling
At the heart and soul.

The strong arms
That held me up
When my own strength
Let me down
Each morsel that I was
Fed with was full of love divine.

At every turning of my life
I came across
Good friends
Friends who stood by me
Even when the time raced me by.

Farewell
Farewell
My friends
I smile and
Bid you goodbye
No, shed no tears
For I need them not
All I need is your smile.

If you feel sad
Do think of me
For that's what I like
When you live in the hearts
Of those you love
Remember then . . .
You never die.

Gitanjali

22   All my friends
Are coming up to death –
All is separation;
Gone affection
And a heart's comforts,
The little remembered gifts
And laughter over spring-time meals at nine.

All my friends
Are coming up to death –
All is parting;
Vanished loving
And the eyes' joys,
The shared evocative rambles
And music on late summer nights.

All my friends
Are coming up to death –
All is farewell;

Lost tenderness
And a mind's tussles,
The tense and struggling arguments
Over books read as autumn closes in.

All my friends
Are coming up to death –
All is forgiveness;
Forgotten now betrayals
And the petty, small mistakes
The fallibility of tongues and deeds
As Christ and his thief touch our dark and winter lives.

Brian Frost

23

I don't believe in Death
Who mocks in silent stealth;
He robs us only of a breath,
Not of a life-time's wealth.

I don't believe the tomb
Imprisons us in earth;
It's but another loving womb
Preparing our new birth.

I do believe in Life
Empowered from above;
Till, freed from stress and worldly strife,
We soar through realms of love.

I do believe that then,
In joy that never ends,
We'll meet all those we've loved, again,
And celebrate our friends.

Pauline Webb

Sources and Acknowledgments

Definitions

2 Aristotle (384–322 BC), *Ethics*, taken from the Penguin 1953 edition translated by J. A. K. Thomson.

3, 4 Cicero (106–43 BC), *De Amicitia*.

5 Joseph Zabara, *Sefer Shaashuim* (thirteenth century.)

6 Abel Bonnard (1883–1968), French writer of travel books. From 'The Art of Friendship', part ii.

7, 8 Jeremy Taylor (1613–67), 'A Discourse of the Nature, Measure and Offices of Friendship', 1657.

9 Feast Day Sermon at St Mary-Le-Bow, London, 1 December 1684.

10 William Penn (1644–1718), 'Some Fruits of Solitude', 1693.

11 Oliver Goldsmith (1730–1774), *The Good Natured Man*, 1767.

12 Samuel Johnson (1709–1784). Quoted by James Boswell in his *Life of Samuel Johnson*, 1775.

13 Samuel Taylor Coleridge (1772–1834), 'Youth and Age'.

15 Thomas Jefferson (1743–1826), *Writings*, Vol 13.

16 George Eliot (1819–1889), *Daniel Deronda*, 1876.

17 Ralph Waldo Emerson (1803–1882), 'Friendship', *Essays*, First Series, 1841.

18 Dag Hammarskjøld, *Markings*, Faber 1964.

19 Nadir Dinshaw, *Love in Friendship*, privately published 1984. Used by permission.

20, 21 John Kasmin, 'Men and Friends', interview in the *Observer* supplement, 26 January 1986.

23 Shelley Winters, reported in *The New York Times*, 18 June 1976.

24 Katharine Whitehorn, 'My Best Friend Once Removed', *Sunday Best*, Eyre Methuen 1981.

26 Jill Tweedie, from an article in *The Guardian*, 12 January 1970.

Celebrations

1 Contributed by Mr Leslie Sherwood from a calendar *c.*1905 and used with permission.

2 Sappho (b. 612 BC), 'My lovely friends', from Mary Barnard, *Sappho: A New Translation*, University of California Press 1958 (© 1958 by The Regents of the University of California and renewed 1986 by Mary Barnard). Used by permission.

3 'True Friendship', from *The Panchatantra* (second century BC), Sanskrit Scriptures.

4 Aristotle, *Ethics*.

5 Cicero, *De Amicitia*.

6 Augustine of Hippo (354–430), writing about his friends.

7 Po Chu-i (772–846), 'Dreaming that I went with Li and Yü' from Arthur Waley, *More Translations from the Chinese*, Allen and Unwin 1946.

8 Solomon Ibn Gabirol, from *Mibhar Ha Peninim*, *c.* 1050.

9 Francis Bacon (1561–1626), 'Of Friendship', *Essays*, 1625.

10 Christopher Marlowe (1564–1593), *Tamburlaine*, Act I, Sc 2.

11 William Penn, 'Some Fruits of Solitude'.

12 George Herbert (1593–1633), *Jacula Prudentum* (a collection of foreign proverbs in translation), 1651.

13 Robert Burns (1759–1796), 'Auld Lang Syne'.

15 Matthew Arnold (1822–1888), 'Empedocles on Etna'.

16 Henry Thoreau (1817–1862), last two stanzas of the poem 'Friendship'.

17 Ralph Waldo Emerson, 'Friendship', *Essays*, First Series, 1841.

18 Walt Whitman (1819–1892), 'We Two Boys Clinging Together', *Complete Poetry and Selected Essays* ed Emory Holloway, Nonesuch Press 1938.

19 Kahlil Gibran (1883–1931), *The Prophet*, Heinemann 1926.

20 J. K. Aggrey (1875–1927), 'Friendship'. Translation of a French original by Eugene De Loulay.

21 The Oglala Sioux Indians, from Thomas E. Sanders, *The Literature of the American Indians*, Collier-Macmillan 1973.

22 Winifred Holtby (1898–1935), 'I owe so large a debt to life' from Vera Brittain, *Testament of Friendship*, Macmillan 1940. Used by permission.

23 Hilaire Belloc (1870–1953), from 'Dedicatory Ode', *Sonnets and Verse*, Duckworth 1910. Used with the permission of A. D. Peters and Co.

24 Gwyn Williams, 'Aspects of Now', *Foundation Stock*, Gomer 1974. Used by permission.

25 Michael Macnamara, '15–45', from the poetry magazine *Ophir*, No 17 (June 1973). Used by permission of the author.

28 Thomas McGrath, 'Letter to an Imaginary Friend' in *Poets of Today – A New American Anthology* ed Walter Lowenfels, International Publishing Co, NY 1964. Used by permission of the publisher.

Hospitality

1 Ralph Waldo Emerson, 'Domestic Life', an extract from *Society and Solitude*, 1870.

3 Meng Hao-jan (689–740), 'On stopping at an old friend's homestead' from *300 T'ang Poems* translated by Innes Herdan, The Far East Book Company, Taiwan 1970. Copies may be obtained from Mrs Innes Herdan, 81A Gloucester Avenue, London NW1 8LB.

4 Tu Fu (712–770), 'For Mr Wei, a Retired Scholar' from *300 T'ang Poems*.

5 Ssu-k'ung Shu (eighth century), 'Parting from Han Shen' from *300 T'ang Poems*.

6 Ben Jonson (1572–1637), 'Inviting a Friend to Supper'.

7 Kenneth Macleod, 'The Celtic Rune of Hospitality'. Quoted on a motto card and used by permission of The Iona Community.

8 David Williams, 'We Shook Hands', *Christian*, Easter 1983. Used by

permission of the Editor.

9 Henri Nouwen, *Reaching Out*, Doubleday 1975.
10 W. H. Auden (1907–1973), 'For Friends Only', *About the House*, Faber 1966. Used by permission.
11 Svetlana Alliluyeva, *Twenty Letters to a Friend*, Hutchinson 1967. Used by permission of A. W. Watt.
12 C. Day-Lewis (1904–1972), 'At Lemmons', *Poems of C. Day-Lewis 1925–1972*, Jonathan Cape 1977. Used by permission.
13 Sister Emmanuelle, *Sister with the Ragpickers*, Triangle/SPCK 1982. Used by permission.
14 James Cameron (1911–1985), 'Celebrating Divali Together', *The Guardian*, 30 October 1984. Used by permission of Mrs Moni Cameron.
15 Alison Head, from *Reflection on Revelation I*. Used with the author's permission.

Candour

1 Ovid (43BC–AD18), *Tristia*, Book I.
2, 3 Aristotle, *Ethics*.
4 William Shakespeare (1564–1616), *Julius Caesar*, Act IV, Sc 2.
5 William Shakespeare, *Hamlet*, Act I, Sc 3.
6 Honein Ben Isaak, *Moral Maxims*. Honein Ben Isaak was an Arab moralist, *c.* AD 870.
7 William Blake (1757–1827), 'The Marriage of Heaven and Hell', 1790.
8, 9 William Blake, 'Jerusalem', 1804.
10 William Blake, 'Notebook 1808–11'.
11 Giordano Bruno (1548–1600). An Italian philosopher.
12 Alfred, Lord Tennyson (1809–1892), 'Elaine', 1859, one of *The Idylls of the King*.
13, 14 Charlotte Brontë (1816–1855), quoted in Mrs Gaskell's *Life of Charlotte Brontë*, 1857.
15 Thomas De Quincey (1785–1859), 'On Schlosser's Literary History'.
16, 17 Ralph Waldo Emerson, 'Friendship', *Essays*, First Series, 1841.
18 Mark Twain (1835–1910), *Notebook*, 1935.
19 Churton Collins (1848–1908), Aphorisms in the *The English Review*, 1914.
20 E. M. Forster (1879–1970), *Two Cheers for Democracy*, Arnold 1951.
21 G. K. Chesterton (1874–1936), English essayist, critic, novelist and poet.
22 Friedrich Nietzsche, (1844–1900) *Thus Spoke Zarathustra*, Penguin 1961.
23 Hugh Kingsmill (1899–1949), literary critic and biographer. From *The Best of Hugh Kingsmill* ed Michael Holroyd, Gollancz 1970.
24 Ethel Watts Mumford (1878–1940), American writer.
25 David Head, *He Sent Leanness*, Epworth Press 1959. Used by permission.
26 Aldous Huxley (1894–1963), *Brave New World*, Chatto and Windus 1932.
27 Maxim Ghilan, 'To an Old Friend' in *An Anthology of Modern Hebrew Poetry*, Abelard/Schumann 1968. Used with the permission of the author.
29 Max Plowman (1883–1941), *Bridge Into the Future*, Dakers 1944. Plowman was a leader in the Peace Pledge Union.
31 Laurence Housman (1865–1959). *The Unexpected Years*, Jonathan Cape 1937. Used by permission.

32 Douglas Steere, 'Where Words Come From', Swarthmore Lecture 1955, published in Britain by the Quaker Home Service Committee and reissued in 1985. Used with the permission of the author.

33 Ivor Smith-Cameron, 'Some thoughts on the art of friendship'. Privately printed paper, available from the author at 25 The Chase, London SW4, and used by permission.

34 Nadir Dinshaw, *Love in Friendship*, privately published 1984. Used by permission.

35 Mary O'Hara, *Celebration of Love*, Hodder 1985. Used with the permission of the author.

36 Carole Etzler, 'Distances', *Feminist Songs*, published by Sanray Sisters Music Unlimited (EMI 1976).

37 Langston Hughes, 'Poem', *The Dream Keeper and Other Poems*, © 1932 by Alfred A. Knopf Inc. and renewed 1960 by Langston Hughes. Reprinted by permission of Alfred A. Knopf Inc.

38 John Steinbeck (1902–1968), *East of Eden*, Heinemann 1952.

39 Albert Camus, (1913–1960) *Lyrical and Critical*, Hamish Hamilton 1961. Used with permission.

Love

1 Lord Byron's translation of a French Proverb, 'L'amitié est l'amour sans ailes'.

2 Emily Brontë (1818–1848), 'Love and Friendship'.

3, 4 John Masefield (1878–1967). 'Being Her Friend' and 'The Word' are used with the permission of The Society of Authors as the literary representative of the Estate of John Masefield.

5 Elizabeth Jennings, 'Friendship' from *New Poems 1970–71*, a PEN anthology of contemporary poetry ed Alan Brownjohn, Seamus Heaney and Jon Stall-worthy, Hutchinson 1971. Used with the permission of the author.

6 Harry Lee, 'To a Friend' from Leslie Weatherhead, *A Private House of Prayer*, Hodder 1958.

7 Anna Akhmatova (1889–1966), from a poem in *White Flock* included in *Selected Poems* translated by Richard McKane, OUP and Penguin. Used by permission.

8 Boris Pasternak (1890–1960), 'Meeting', *In the Interlude: Poems 1945–60*, OUP 1962. Used with the permission of A. D. Peters and Co.

9 George Buchanan, 'I Suddenly' in *Poets of Northern Ireland* ed Frank Ormsby, Blackstone Press 1979.

10 Leonard Cohen, 'Do Not Forget Old Friends', *Collected Poems 1956–1968*, Jonathan Cape 1969. Used by permission.

11 Sydney Carter, 'Love from Manchester', *Nothing Fixed or Final*, Galliard 1969. Used with the permission of the author and of Stainer and Bell.

12 Bruce Lansdale, BBC World Service *Reflections* script, February 1985. Used with the permission of the author.

13 Abbas Husain, 'Our Friendship'. Previously unpublished. Used with the permission of the author.

14 Mary Wollstonecraft (1759–1797), 'Vindication of the Rights of Woman', 1792.

15 Friedrich Nietzsche, from *The Nietzsche–Wagner correspondence* ed Elizabeth Foefster-Nietzsche, Duckworth 1922. Used by permission.

16 C. S. Lewis (1898–1963), *The Four Loves*, Collins 1963. Used by permission.

17 Elizabeth Hannon, from an unpublished piece prepared for the World Council of Churches' Vancouver Assembly and used with the author's permission.

18 Herbert Hensley Henson (1863–1947), *Letters of Herbert Hensley Henson*, chosen and edited by Evelyn Foley Braley, SPCK 1951.

19 Simone Weil, *Waiting on God*, Routledge and Kegan Paul 1952. Used by permission.

Cameos

1 Samuel Johnson (1709–1784): taken from Leslie Stephen, *Johnson*, 1888.

2 Jane Austen (1775–1817): taken from David Cecil, *Portrait of Jane Austen*, Constable 1978. Used by permission.

3 William Pitt (1759–1806): taken from Earl Stanhope's *Life of William Pitt*, 1861.

4 John Keats (1795–1821): taken from *Keat's Letters* Vol 2, ed Hyder Rollins, CUP 1958.

5 Charles Dickens (1812–1870): taken from John Forster's *Life of Dickens*, 1872–4.

6 William Gladstone (1809–1898): taken from *The Gladstone Diaries* ed M. R. D. Foot and H. C. G. Matthew, Clarendon Press 1968.

7 Oscar Wilde (1854–1900): taken from Richard le Gallienne, *The Romantic Nineties*, Putnam and Co 1951.

8 Nietzsche (1844–1900) and Wagner (1813–1883): taken from Friedrich Nietzsche, *Joyful Wisdom* (Collected Works, Vol 10), Duckworth 1922. Used by permission.

9 Friedrich von Hügel (1852–1925), Roman Catholic theologian and philosopher: taken from Gwendolene Greene's Introduction to *Letters from Baron von Hügel to a Niece*, Dent 1928. Used by permission.

10 Sigmund Freud (1856–1939): taken from Marthe Robert, *The Psychoanalytic Revolution*, Allen and Unwin 1966. Used by permission.

11 Carl Jung (1875–1961): taken from Laurens van der Post, *Jung and the Story of our Time*, Hogarth Press 1976. Used by permission.

12 The Bloomsbury Group (Virginia and Leonard Woolf, Maynard Keynes, Clive and Vanessa Bell, Lytton Strachey): taken from A. L. Gadd, *The Loving Friends*, Hogarth Press 1974. Used by permission.

13 Winifred Holtby (1898–1935): taken from Vera Brittain, *Testament of Friendship*, Macmillan 1940. Used by permission.

14 Hilaire Belloc (1870–1953): taken from G. K. Chesterton's *Autobiography*, Hutchinson 1937.

15 Lucy Menzies (author of devotional books): taken from Lumsden Barkway's Memoir of Lucy Menzies in Margaret Cropper, *Evelyn Underhill*, Longmans 1958. Used by permission.

16 Hugh Kingsmill (1889–1949): taken from Malcolm Muggeridge, *Tread Softly for You Tread on My Jokes*, Collins 1966. Used by permission.

17 C. F. Andrews (1871–1940), missionary priest in India: taken from Hugh

Tinker, *The Ordeal of Love*, OUP India 1979. Used by permission.

18 E. M. Forster (1879–1970): taken from P. N. Furbank, *E. M. Forster: A Life*, Secker and Warburg 1977. Used by permission.

19 Studdert Kennedy (1883–1929): taken from *G. A. Studdert Kennedy by his friends* ed J. K. Mozley, Hodder 1929. The writer is H. R. L. Sheppard. Used by permission.

20 Paul Tillich (1886–1965): taken from Rollo May, *Paulus*, Collins 1974. Used by permission.

21 Dietrich Bonhoeffer (1906–1945) and Eberhard Bethge: taken from Mary Bosanquet, *The Life and Death of Dietrich Bonhoeffer*, Hodder 1968. Used by permission.

22 Dick Sheppard (1880–1937): taken from *Dick Sheppard by his friends* ed Howard Marshall and used with the permission of the literary executor of Rose Macaulay.

23 Mahatma Gandhi (1869–1948): taken from Margaret Chatterjee, *Gandhi's Religious Thought*, Macmillan 1983. Used by permission.

24 Winston Churchill (1874–1965) and Violet Bonham Carter (1887–1969): taken from Violet Bonham Carter, *Winston Churchill as I Knew Him*, Collins 1965. Used by permission.

25 Eleanor Roosevelt (1884–1962): taken from Joseph P. Lash, *The Years Alone*, André Deutsch 1973, quoting a comment by Mrs Roosevelt to David Gurewitsch.

26 Aneurin Bevan (1897–1960): taken from Michael Foot, MP, *Aneurin Bevan* Vol 1, Macgibbon and Kee 1962, and used with the author's permission.

27 Hugh Gaitskell: taken from *Hugh Gaitskell 1906–1963* ed W. T. Rodgers, Thames and Hudson 1964, and used with the permission of the writer, The Rt Hon Roy Jenkins, MP.

28 Iain Macleod (1913–1970): taken from Nigel Fisher, *Iain Macleod*, André Deutsch 1973.

29 Lord Beaverbrook (1879–1964): taken from Nadir Dinshaw, *Love in Friendship*, privately published 1984. Used by permission.

30 Nelson Mandela and Oliver Tambo: taken from Mary Benson, *Nelson Mandela*, Penguin 1986. The quotation from Oliver Tambo's Introduction to *No Easy Walk to Freedom* is used by permission of Heinemann Educational Books.

31 Steve Biko (1946–1977): taken from Donald Woods, *Biko*, Paddington Press 1978. Used by permission.

32 Dylan Thomas (1914–1953): taken from Dylan Thomas, *Letters to Vernon Watkins*, Dent 1957. Used with permission of the publisher and David Higham Associates Ltd.

33 Marlene Dietrich and Ernest Hemingway (1899–1961): taken from A. E. Hotchner, *Papa Hemingway*, Weidenfeld and Nicolson 1970. Used by permission.

34 Joyce Grenfell (1910–1979): taken from *Joyce by herself and her friends*, Macmillan 1980. Used with the permission of Virginia Graham.

35 The Inklings (C. S. Lewis, J. R. R. Tolkein, Charles Williams and their friends): taken from Humphrey Carpenter, *The Inklings*, Allen and Unwin 1978. Used by permission.

36 Sybil Thorndike (1882–1976): taken from John Casson, *Lewis and Sybil: A Memoir*, Collins 1979. Used by permission.

Conflict

1 Mahatma Gandhi (1869–1948), *Collected Works*, Navajivan Trust, Bombay, India.

2 Wang-Chien (late eighth/ early nineteenth century), 'Hearing that his friend was coming back from the war' in *Chinese Poems* translated by Arthur Waley, Allen and Unwin 1919. Used by permission.

3 Cicero, *Letters to his Friends II* translated by Glynn Williams, Loeb Classical Library, Heinemann 1929.

4 Robert Bolt, *A Man for All Seasons*, Heinemann 1967. Used by permission.

5 American Quaker Report, *Speak Truth to Power*, American Friends Service Committee, *c.* 1955.

6 Martin Luther King (1929–1968), *Strength to Love*, Hodder 1964. Used with the permission of the publisher and the Estate of Martin Luther King, Jr.

7 Mahatma Gandhi, *Collected Works*, Navajivan Trust, Bombay, India.

8 Henry Lawson, *Vignettes from the Western Front: Reflections of an Infantry Subaltern in France 1917/18*, published for the Friends of Guildford Cathedral by Positif Press, Oxford 1979. Used with the permission of the family of the late Sir Henry Lawson.

9 Alexander Solzhenitsyn, *The First Circle*, Collins 1968. Used by permission.

10 William Shawcross, *Dubcek*, Weidenfeld and Nicolson 1970. Used by permission.

11 Coretta Scott King, *My Life with Martin Luther King, Jr*, Hodder 1970. Used by permission.

12 Dennis Brutus, from 'For Chief – A Tribute to Albert Luthuli', *A Simple Lust*, Heinemann 1973. Used by permission.

13 Canaan Banana, 'A Friend in Need', *The Gospel According to the Ghetto*, Mambo Press, Zimbabwe 1980. Used with the permission of His Excellency the President of Zimbabwe.

14 Mervyn Morris, 'To An Expatriate Friend', *The Pond*, New Beacon Books Ltd 1973. Used by permission.

15 Zephania Kameeta, *Why, O Lord?* Psalms and sermons from Namibia, WCC 1986. Used by permission.

16 C. Adel, 'Azucena our Sister' in *Poems of the Mothers of the Plaza de Mayo*, published 1983 by Busqueda and obtainable from 77 Old High Street, Headington, Oxford. Used by permission. C. Adel was one of the women who silently protested about the disappearance of members of their families in the Argentine during the period of military rule.

17 Dorothee Sölle, *Revolutionary Patience*, Orbis Books, Maryknoll, NY 1977. Used with the permission of the author.

18 Carole Etzler, 'Sometimes I wish', *Feminist Songs*, Sanray Sisters Music Unlimited (EMI 1976).

19 Angela Tilby, *Won't You Join the Dance?*, SPCK 1985. Used by permission.

Faith

1 Aelred of Rievaulx (1109–1167), *Spiritual Friendship*.

2 Sarojimi Chourdney, quoted in B. Chaturvedi and M. Sykes, *C. F. Andrews: A Biography*, Allen and Unwin 1948.

3 Henry Thoreau, *Treatise on Friendship*.

4 Max Plowman, *Bridge into the Future*, Dakers 1944.

5–12 The extracts from the Authorized King James Version of the Bible, which is Crown Copyright in the United Kingdom, are reproduced by permission of Eyre and Spottiswoode (Publishers) Ltd, Her Majesty's Printers, London.

The extracts from the Apocrypha are taken from the New English Bible, Second Edition, © 1970, and used with the permission of the Oxford and Cambridge University Presses.

13 Stephen Neill, *A Genuinely Human Existence*, Doubleday and Co Inc, NY 1959. Reprinted by permission.

14 Jürgen Moltmann, *The Open Church*, SCM Press 1978. Used by permission.

15 Gerald Vann, OP, *The High Green Hill*, Collins 1951. Used by permission.

16 R. O. Hall (1895–1975), quoted by David Paton in *The Life and Times of Bishop Hall of Hong Kong*, Diocese of Hong Kong and Macao and the Hong Kong Diocesan Association 1985. Used with the permission of Canon A. C. Hall.

17 Ivor Smith-Cameron, 'Some thoughts on the art of friendship', privately printed paper. Used with the author's permission.

18 Lope de Vega (1562–1635), 'What do I have, that you seek out my friendship?' in *An Anthology of Spanish Poetry from Garcilaso to Garcia Lorca*, Doubleday 1961, © Angel Flores 1961. Used by permission.

19 Jeremy Taylor, 'A Discourse of the Nature, Measure and Offices of Friendship', 1657.

20 François Fénelon (1651–1715), 'Explication des maximes des saintes sur la vie interieure',1697.

21 Pierre Ceresole (1879–1945), 'For Peace and Truth' from *The Notebooks of Pierre Ceresole*, Bannisdale Press 1954. Ceresole was the founder of the International Voluntary Service.

22 Jürgen Moltmann, *The Open Church*, SCM Press 1978. Used by permission.

23 Thomas Kelly (1893–1941), *A Testament of Devotion*, Harper and Row 1941. Used by permission.

24 Charles Wesley (1708–1788), from *A Collection of Hymns for the Use of the People called Methodists*, published by John Wesley in 1780.

25 Anthony Bridge, BBC World Service *Reflections* script, 1986. Used with permission.

26 Prue Wilson, *My Father Took Me to The Circus*, Darton Longman and Todd 1984. Used with permission.

27 Eric James, *The House of My Friends*, Christian Action 1984. Used with permission.

28 Fynn, *Mister God, This is Anna*, Collins 1974. Used with permission.

Endings

2 Cicero, 'Essay on Old Age' translated in *Offices, Essays on Friendship and Old Age and Select Letters*, Dent 1909.

3 Al-Khansa (?590–644?) 'Lament for a Brother' in *Arabic and Persian Poems* translated by Omar Pound, Fulcrum Press 1970.

4 Li Po (701–762), 'Taking leave of a friend' in *300 T'ang Poems*.

5 William Shakespeare, Sonnet XXX.

6 John Bunyan (1628–1688), *Pilgrims Progress*, Part II, 1684.

7 Henry Vaughan (1622–1695), 'They are all gone into the world of light'.

8 William Penn, 'More Fruits of Solitude', 1702.

9 Charles Wesley: from *A Collection of Hymns for the Use of the People called Methodists*.

10 Felicia Dorothea Hemans (1793–1835), 'Dirge' from *The Siege of Valencia*.

11 Lord Byron (1788–1824), 'Thomas More'.

12 Henry Austin Dobson (1840–1924), 'Fame and Friendship'.

13 Alfred, Lord Tennyson, 'Break, break, break'.

14 Robert Browning (1812–1889), 'May and Death'.

15 William Cory (1823–1892), 'Heraclitus'.

16 A. E. Housman (1859–1936), *Collected Poems*, Jonathan Cape 1936. Used with the permission of the publisher and of The Society of Authors as the Executor of the Literary Estate of A. E. Housman.

17 John Betjeman (1906–1984), 'Old Friends' in *Collected Poems*, John Murray 1970. Used by permission.

18 Rabindranath Tagore (1861–1941), in *Some Songs and Poems from Rabindranath Tagore* translated by Pratina Bowes, East/West Publications 1984. Used by permission.

19 Awang Kedua, 'On hearing of a friend's death' in *An Anthology of Contemporary Malaysian Literature* 1930–1963 ed T. Wignesan, Raybooks, Kuala Lumpur 1964.

20 José Hernandez (1834–1886), Argentinian Poet. 'The departure of Martin Fierro' in *The Gaucho Martin Fierro* translated by Walter Owen, Farrer and Rinehart 1936.

21 Gitanjali, 'Farewell my friends' in *Poems of Gitanjali*, Oriel Press 1982. Used with the permission of the publishers and of the copyright holder, Khushi Badruddin.

22 Brian Frost, 'All my friends', previously unpublished.

23 Pauline Webb, 'I don't delieve in Death', previously unpublished.